Paddy Hopkirk says:

'Sooner or later, every car owner faces the ruinous cost of servicing, maintaining and repairing his car. That's why more and more car owners are turning to DIY methods as the only way of slashing motoring costs.

PITMAN'S ALL-IN-ONE motoring books are written by professional motoring writers who understand car owners' needs.
The books have been specially designed to give all the information needed, in clear diagrams, trouble-shooting charts, photographs and easy-to-follow text, making it easy for DIY car owners to keep costs of motoring at rock bottom.

Whatever the car owner's approach to home servicing – whether as a novice or an expert – PITMAN'S ALL-IN-ONE motoring books offer him for the first time a combined maintenance handbook and workshop manual – all the DIY car owner needs to get the best out of his car.'

Paddy Hopkirk

The two most popular models in the Minor range are the saloon (upper picture) and the Traveller estate car version (below). In addition the Tourer (convertible) and the van had large sales

All-in-one
book of the
Morris Minor 1000
Staton Abbey

A maintenance, fault-tracing and home workshop manual

Covering the Minor 1000 from October 1956
948 cc and 1098 cc models
Saloon
Tourer
Traveller
Van

Pitman

First published 1977

UK
Pitman Publishing Ltd
Pitman House, 39 Parker Street, London, WC2B 5PB

Pitman Medical Publishing Co Ltd
42 Camden Road, Tunbridge Wells, Kent, TN1 2QD

Focal Press Ltd
31 Fitzroy Square, London, W1P 6BH

USA
Pitman Publishing Corporation
6 East 43 Street, New York, NY 10017

Fearon Publishers Inc
6 Davis Drive, Belmont California 94002

AUSTRALIA
Pitman Publishing Pty Ltd
Pitman House, 158 Bouverie Street, Carlton, Victoria 3053

CANADA
Pitman Publishing
Copp Clark Publishing
517 Wellington Street West, Toronto, M5V 1GL

EAST AFRICA
Sir Isaac Pitman and Sons Ltd
Banda Street, PO Box 46038, Nairobi, Kenya

SOUTH AFRICA
Pitman Publishing Co (SA) Pty Ltd
Craighall Mews, Jan Smuts Avenue, Craighall Park,
Johannesburg 2001

ISBN 0 273 010 69 7

Designed & illustrated by Design Practitioners Ltd
Set in Univers light by Type Practitioners Ltd
Reproduced and printed by photolithography and bound in
Great Britain at The Pitman Press, Bath

Contents

Acknowledgements

Many firms and individuals have helped in the preparation of this book. Among those to whom special thanks are due are —

Leyland Cars Service and Parts Division
Automotive Products Co Ltd
Champion Sparking Plug Co Ltd
AE Edmunds Walker Ltd
Holt Products Ltd
Joseph Lucas Ltd
SU Carburettors

The greatest care has been taken to check and cross-check the information and servicing data, but liability cannot be accepted for errors or omissions, or for changes in specifications that are sometimes introduced by a manufacturer during the production run of a model.

Part one

1 Before you begin
How this series was planned

Are you a dedicated do-it-yourself enthusiast — or an owner with only limited practical experience, forced by continually rising costs to maintain and repair your car at home?

Whatever your approach to home servicing — whether as a novice or as an expert — the handbooks in this series have been tailored to meet your needs and abilities. Each forms a combined, all-in-one maintenance handbook and home workshop manual, with the emphasis solidly on the practical aspects of the work.

We introduce you to your car, advise you how to vet a used example, tell you how to get it through the Ministry test and take you progressively through preventive maintenance, trouble-shooting, servicing, repairs and overhauls.

We have made the workshop manual chapters as comprehensive as possible, while bearing in mind the less than ideal conditions under which the average owner must usually carry out repairs and overhauls. But it must be accepted that some jobs are outside the province of the home mechanic; they call for the use of special workshop tools and equipment and — in many cases — for special skills.

Botched-up repairs can be dangerous and we feel strongly that owners should not be encouraged to do work which might entail safety risks.

How this book is arranged

In Part One you will find an in-depth study of the models covered, together with information on servicing and preventive maintenance. We take the logical view that it is better to avoid trouble than to try to put it right after it has developed.

Even the most meticulous maintenance, however, cannot guarantee freedom from faults, so we have included in Part Two a comprehensive set of trouble-tracing charts which should enable you to pin-point a trouble quickly and accurately.

If your car is due for the Ministry test, the tips that we give should enable it to pass with flying colours. Many cars fail quite unnecessarily, due to faults which could have been put right by a practical owner.

While still on the theme of putting your car in tip-top condition, we tell you how to tackle rust and bodywork blemishes and how to restore a showroom shine.

The remainder of the book forms a concise home workshop manual, covering all the jobs that can be safely tackled without the need for elaborate equipment, and supported by comprehensive specifications and data tables.

The practical aspects

We have tried to anticipate your difficulties and to give practical pointers and advice where necessary. For example, would it be quicker and cheaper to fit a new or fully-reconditioned part instead of stripping and repairing a worn component? When should the help of a specialist repair firm be enlisted? We give you the pros and cons (and the economics) of these problems, to help you to make an informed decision.

Time is often a vital factor and we have included in the workshop manual chapters what we think are some realistic times for the more important jobs and major operations. We have erred on the generous side, bearing in mind the needs of the novice, but it would be wise to allow an additional safety margin to take care of unexpected snags. The times that we suggest, therefore, will not necessarily agree with those that may be quoted by a British Leyland dealer, who has a well-equipped workshop and racks full of expensive special tools.

Finally, we have broken down the servicing and overhaul instructions into simple step-by-step sequences which are exceptionally easy to follow and should give a beginner the confidence to tackle fairly ambitious work.

Where there are snags, we don't hesitate to say so. And where special service tools are needed, we list them.

As for the work itself, that is — literally — in your hands. We hope that we shall have helped to make it a little easier.

2 Getting to know your car
Facts and figures

When the first post-war Morris Minor was introduced in 1948, it immediately acquired an enviable reputation as a small, inexpensive family saloon that also appealed to the sporting driver, having sensitive steering and excellent handling qualities.

The introduction of an overhead-valve engine in 1952 was a welcome improvement on the somewhat unenterprising 918 cc side-valve engine fitted to the first models, but much of the benefit of the new power unit was offset, from the enthusiast's point of view, by the smaller capacity of the engine (803 cc) and the introduction at the same time of a lower-geared rear axle and a gearbox with more widely spaced ratios.

Not until the Minor 1000 was announced in October 1956, with a 948 cc overhead-valve engine, close-ratio gearbox and 4.5:1 rear axle, were the full potentialities of the car realized. Moreover, the new engine had been the subject of considerable development, including prolonged high-speed tests on German motor roads, during which prototypes had averaged over 60 mph for 25 000 miles.

At the 1962 London Motor Show the 1098 cc model was introduced. The larger engine gave the car a still better performance and greater flexibility in top gear. At the same time the manufacturers took the wise step of installing rear-axle gears which had a slightly higher ratio, thus cutting down the engine revs and ensuring more restful cruising at higher speeds.

From then onwards, until the last Minor — a Traveller — was phased-out early in 1971, only detail changes were made, the most important of which are listed at the end of this chapter.

The engine

The robust little Leyland 'A' series engine will be familiar to many readers, having proved its worth in a wide range of cars, including the Minis, the 1100/1300 and the Midget and Sprite models. It has been adapted for front-wheel-drive and also used with conventional front-engine, rear-wheel-drive layouts, as in the Minor. The engine components are described in Chapter 9 and full specifications are given in Chapter 17.

In the Minor 1000 the basic power unit has a capacity of either 948 cc or 1098 cc. The simple push-rod overhead-valve design provides no headaches as far as maintenance and repair are concerned, even quite ambitious overhauls being possible without removing it from the car.

Spares are easy to find, many being interchangeable with those used in similar installations in other Leyland models. It is even possible to fit a 1098 cc power unit in place of a 948 cc engine, with only detail changes to various ancillary items such as pipes and wiring.

The transmission

A conventional Borg and Beck single-plate clutch is fitted to all models. The clutch release is controlled by a cable, instead of by an hydraulic cylinder as used with most other Leyland cars.

The earlier synchromesh gearbox incorporates a 'constant-pressure' type of synchromesh on the three upper gears and calls for a fairly leisurely change to avoid crunching the gears, even when the synchromesh cones are in good condition. When shopping around, therefore, it would pay to choose a 1098 cc model, as these cars are fitted with baulk-ring synchromesh which provides a much more positive change, although bottom gear remains unsynchronized as on the earlier cars.

The gearbox is linked to the conventional 'live' rear axle by an open propeller shaft which has a needle-roller universal joint at each end.

Since provision is made for regular lubrication of these joints, they should normally last much longer than the so-called 'sealed for life' joints fitted to most modern cars. Also — unlike the majority of present-day joints — they can be overhauled when the needle-roller bearings become worn.

Suspension and steering

The light, precise handling and excellent controllability which characterized the Minor from its inception in 1948, can largely be attributed to the torsion-bar front suspension and the rack-and-pinion steering gear.

The base of the swivel pin that carries each front-wheel hub is connected by a screwed link pin to the outer end of a lower suspension arm, which is pivoted in rubber bushes at its inner end where it is attached to a steel torsion bar which carries the load and acts as a spring by twisting throughout its length.

The rear end of each bar is splined into a lever which bears against an adjustable stop on the underframe, allowing the height of the front of the car to be easily trimmed if one bar should 'settle' more than the other.

The upper suspension arm is formed by the lever of

an hydraulic, piston-type shock absorber. The outer end of this lever is coupled to the top of the swivel-pin assembly.

At the rear, conventional semi-elliptic leaf springs are used, damped by lever-type shock absorbers. This simple arrangement provides a good ride, although the rear axle is not so positively located as in the majority of modern rear-suspension layouts and this can result in axle-tramp when accelerating hard in the lower gears. In normal driving, however, tramp is unlikely to be experienced and the ride and controllability are still good by modern standards.

The brakes

The modest performance of the Minor 1000 — even when fitted with the 1098 cc engine — does not call for the use of disc front brakes or a servo and the Lockheed all-drum layout which is fitted provides quite adequate retardation.

The front brakes are of the two-leading-shoe type, whereas leading and trailing shoes are used in the rear drums. Lubrication nipples are provided on the hand-brake cables and if these receive attention with the grease gun at 6000-mile intervals, seizing-up of the cables — a common fault on the Series II and earlier Minors — should not be experienced.

The one poor feature of the braking system is the fact that the master cylinder is mounted beneath the floor of the driver's compartment, which means that any leakage of fluid past the seals is less likely to be spotted quickly, and also that the carpet must be lifted in order to reach the reservoir plug, with the risk of dirt or grit falling into the reservoir when the level is being topped-up.

Model line-up

Now for a list of some of the more important stages in the development of the Minor 1000. These details will be useful in 'dating' a used car, but remember that changes were sometimes made gradually during the production run of a model, as parts became available on the assembly line.

Also, completed cars often spent some time at the factory awaiting collection, followed by a further period in dealers' showroooms before they were sold. Consequently the date of registration is not always a guarantee that a modification has been incorporated.

The other side of the picture, of course, is that keen owners of a car like the Minor, which appeals to the d.i.y. enthusiast, often spend a lot of time bringing their cars up to the later specifications. Even complete engine and gearbox swaps are not unusual. This can be a useful bonus for a subsequent buyer, of course, but it does emphasize the need to treat the 'official' modification list with some reserve.

The mechanical specifications of the vans broadly followed those of the cars, but with detailed changes in some cases to meet the requirements of specialist users.

1956, October. Series II Morris Minor replaced by the Minor 1000 two-door and four-door saloons, Tourer (convertible) and Traveller. Similar to previous cars but with one-piece curved windscreens and larger rear windows. Engine capacity increased to 948 cc, producing 35 bhp net at 4800 rpm. Higher rear axle ratio (4.55:1) and closer ratios in gearbox.

1957, April. Petrol-tank capacity increased from 5 gallons to $6\frac{1}{2}$ gallons.

1961, October. Flashing direction indicators fitted in place of semaphore type. Seat-belt anchorages provided and screen washers fitted to de Luxe models.

1962, October. Engine capacity increased to 1098 cc, improving power output to 48 bhp net at 5100 rpm. Baulk-ring synchromesh gearbox gave improved gear-change, but first gear remained unsynchronized. Second gear ratio raised and rear axle ratio changed to 4.3:1.

1963, October. Windscreen wipers changed to parallel operation instead of former 'clap hands' action. Side lamps and flasher lights fitted in combined units.

1964, October. Combined starter and ignition switch replaced separate switches. Other changes included two-spoke steering wheel, oil-filter change warning light (subsequently discontinued), two ashtrays and reintroduction of glove-box lids.

1967, October. Basic models of saloon and Traveller fitted with windscreen washers as standard. Heater and washers provided on de Luxe models.

1969, June. Tourer (convertible) discontinued.

1970, December. Saloons discontinued.

1971, April. Traveller discontinued.

Typical performance figures

We give below some typical performance figures, of which the acceleration times are the most useful in providing an indication of overall efficiency.

Maximum speed should not be held indefinitely, owing to the risk of damaging the engine.

It is difficult to estimate an acceptable fuel consumption figure, the critical factors being the driving conditions and the extent to which the available performance is used.

Model	Maximum speed (mph)	Acceleration 30-50 mph in top gear (seconds)	Average fuel consumption (mpg)
948 cc Saloon or Tourer	74	18	32-42
948 cc Traveller or Van	70	20	30-40
1098 cc Saloon or Tourer	78	14	34-40
1098 cc Traveller or Van	74	16	30-40

3 Vetting a used car
How to detect or forestall trouble

The post-war Morris Minor had a production run of over 22 years — a record rivalled only by the legendary Volkswagen Beetle. As a result, every part was thoroughly tried and tested and the reliability of the Minor became a by-word among family motorists.

Today, even a middle-aged or elderly Minor 1000 can still be an excellent buy on the used-car market, provided that it has been well looked after. Age, of course, must inevitably take its toll, and there must always be some element of risk when buying a used car.

To shorten the odds against you, however, carry out a really thorough check, as suggested in this chapter, before concluding the deal.

If you already own a Minor 1000, a similar check will enable you to decide what work will be needed to put it into tip-top condition.

Fill in an inspection record, on the lines shown on page 18, as you go along. This will be useful later when summing-up the condition of the car and planning the work to be done.

Begin with the bodywork

Take a tip from the motor trade and pay particular attention to the condition of the bodywork. Repairs to rusty or damaged panels, if they are beyond simple home remedies, can be very expensive.

It is best to have the car raised for inspection on a lift, or at least on wheel ramps or on axle stands, so that the underside can be carefully checked.

Rust is likely to show up in the usual places: around the backs of the front and rear wings, in the body sills and in the bottoms of the doors. Fortunately, the front and rear wings are bolted on and for some time at least it should not be too difficult to find spares — although body parts for the Tourer (convertible) have become scarce.

It is particularly important to check for corrosion around the rear-spring mountings, since rust here will result in an MoT test failure. Although repair is possible by welding in new metal, this can be an expensive job.

Also check the battery compartment for corrosion — in this case, caused by spilt acid which can quickly eat through the bulkhead.

With the Traveller there is another source of rot to contend with — dry-rot in the wooden framework of the body, particularly in the horizontal rails where water can lie if the drain holes on the insides of the rails have not been kept open.

Unfortunately, the wood is not used simply as a trim; the parts form the structure of the body to which the metal panels are attached and if rot has got a real hold and spare sections are not available, the only cure is to remove the panels, cut out the affected wooden sections and make up and fit replacements, using glued mortise-and-tenon joints. This should not be beyond the scope of a competent d.i.y. carpenter but will obviously be expensive if the job has to be handed over to a body-repair firm.

Apart from checking for rust and rot, pay special attention to the safety points mentioned on page 12.

Engine condition and performance

We can now turn our attention to the mechanical components, beginning with the engine. This could hardly be more accessible for maintenance and repair, since the engine compartment was originally designed to take a flat-four power unit; but plans for this were scrapped and the conventional side-valve engine used in the previous Series E Morris 8 was substituted in the first post-war Minors. As a result, the equally compact overhead-valve power unit used in the Minor 1000 now sits in splendid isolation in the wide engine bay.

All the Leyland 'A' series engines, including the 948 cc and 1098 cc units used in the Minor 1000, have acquired an enviable reputation for reliability and freedom from minor troubles. It is not unusual for them to run for 60-70 000 miles before the pistons, piston rings and bearings need replacement.

Unless the car has covered a very large mileage, therefore, inspection can be confined to looking for such obvious faults as oil and water leaks, smoke from the exhaust and suspicious noises when the engine is revved-up — check with the engine both hot and cold — followed by a test run during which any misfiring, knocking and lack of power should be evident.

By modern standards these engines are not especially quiet, so don't expect too much. Also, a marked exhaust resonance on the overrun with the throttle closed has always been a feature of the Minor.

A rattling noise at the front of the engine is probably caused by a loose timing chain. A conventional tensioner is not used and the rubber tensioning rings in the sprockets of the earlier engines soon harden — their life seldom exceeds 10 000 miles. The chain then begins to rattle, but provided that the noise is not too loud it is not important — but there is always a risk, of course, that a really badly worn chain may jump a tooth on one of the sprockets and cause fairly extensive engine damage. Fortunately, the chain and sprockets can be renewed without removing the engine and this also applies to the oil seal in the chain cover, if there is oil leakage at this point.

Jot down your observations on your check sheet and at the end of the test compare your notes with the symptoms listed in Trouble-shooting Charts 1-5.

Some cars fitted with the 1098 cc engine suffer from a vibration which comes in at about 20-23 mph in third gear and 30-35 mph in top. This vibration period is not serious and causes no engine damage. The answer is simply to avoid driving in the critical speed ranges as far as possible.

The transmission

The action of the clutch should be smooth. If it slips or does not free completely, resulting in difficult gear-changing, first check that the adjustment of the opera-ting cable is correct — a point which is sometimes overlooked in these days when so many clutches are self-adjusting.

Remember that the synchromesh mechanism used in the gearbox fitted to the 948 cc engines was not of the baulk-ring type and even when new could easily be overridden. When it is worn you will need to learn — or re-learn — the double-declutching technique to obtain clean, quiet changes. If you are prepared to put up with this, however, there is not very much point in going to the expense of fitting a reconditioned gearbox.

The baulk-ring synchromesh used on later (1098 cc) cars is much more satisfactory, but one must accept the fact that like other British Leyland models at that time, the Minor 1000 suffers from the disadvantage of an unsynchronized bottom gear, which means that double-declutching must still be used to ensure a quiet change into first gear when the car is on the move.

Check the drive-line for 'clonks' when the drive is taken up and when opening and closing the throttle. These are most likely to be caused by worn propeller-shaft universal joints, but excessive play in the rear-axle gears cannot be ruled out.

Check the inner sides of the brake backplates for signs of oil leakage from the drain hole at the base of each plate. Leakage here means worn axle seals, and possibly worn rear wheel hub bearings also.

Also check the rear of the gearbox extension and the nose of the rear axle casing for any signs of oil leakage. Renewal of the oil seal in the gearbox or fitting a new seal to the rear axle pinion shaft must be done in the approved manner — and should normally be carried out by a Leyland dealer.

Suspension and steering

As indicated in Chapter 2, the torsion-bar front sus-pension and the rack-and-pinion steering gear set new standards of road-holding and controllability when the post-war Minor was first introduced and although the years may have taken the finer edge off the handling, even by present-day standards the suspen-sion and steering are very good — provided, of course, that the car has been properly maintained and any necessary replacements have been fitted.

Stiff steering or unsatisfactory suspension may be due to nothing more than neglected lubrication of the front suspension pivots and the steering rack. Lubrica-tion nipples are provided at all strategic points, as described in Chapter 14.

The two weak points of the Minor which call for particularly careful checks are the bottom swivels in the front suspension, and the front shock-absorber mountings.

The swivels are of the threaded type and if lubrica-tion has been neglected excessive wear can eventually result in the lower suspension arm parting company with the swivel axle, allowing the wheel to collapse under the car.

The front shock absorber levers act as the upper suspension arms and the resultant stress on the shock absorbers themselves means that the mounting bolts must be kept tight. Although locking tabs are fitted, the bolts always seem to slacken off slightly between services and owners or mechanics are tempted to over-tighten them to prevent a knock from this area. If a bolt has snapped off, it is not an easy job to remove the remaining stub.

Remember that the shock absorbers will be 'tired' when the car has covered about 40 000 miles and will be due for pensioning-off. Fitting new units, however, is well within the scope of a practical owner.

The brakes

As we have indicated in Chapter 2, the Lockheed all-drum hydraulic braking system is more than adequate to cope with the performance of the Minor 1000, provided that the various units are properly maintained and the brakes are correctly adjusted as described in Chapter 15.

If the rear wheels lock-up prematurely when the brakes are applied hard on a smooth road surface, the adjustments of the front and rear brakes are not properly balanced. It is a simple job to put this right.

If the brakes seem to lack power under ordinary driving conditions or the steering pulls to one side, however, Chart 9 will help to pin-point the most likely causes. Fortunately, fitting new brake shoes is neither an expensive nor a difficult job, but if new hydraulic components or brake lines and hoses are likely to be needed, it will be necessary to budget for the cost of these before fixing the price of a used car.

4 Planned servicing
Preventive maintenance

In this and other chapters, we emphasize the importance of *preventive* maintenance — the avoidance of trouble before it becomes serious, or can result in a roadside breakdown.

Your car instruction book specifies servicing at intervals which are determined either by the mileage that has been covered, or by the time that has elapsed, since the last service was carried out. The schedule in this chapter is broadly based on the official servicing scheme, adapted to the needs of the owner who is working at home.

If the car is used mostly for shopping and for an occasional week-end run into the country, for example, the mileage will not accumulate very quickly. While the car is standing idle the contact-breaker gap or the tappet clearances will not be increasing, the brake shoes will not be wearing away and other parts will not require the checks and adjustments called for in the maintenance schedule.

In such cases servicing according to the mileage intervals quoted makes sense. There are cases, however, which justify — for some items — servicing on a time basis rather than by the mileage covered. For example, the engine oil will deteriorate much more quickly when short runs and frequent starts from cold cause excessive condensation of water and acids in the cylinders and sump and will require more frequent changing. The tyres will lose pressure whether the car is running or standing unused and the battery will be subject to slow self-discharge.

The brake fluid slowly absorbs moisture from the air, due to 'breathing' through the vent in the fluid-reservoir filler cap and through slightly porous hoses and the wheel cylinder seals. It will need to be changed after 12-24 months to avoid the risk of brake failure due to the fluid boiling in the wheel cylinders after a spell of hard braking.

The maintenance schedule must therefore be approached in a certain spirit of compromise, depending on the sort of use that the car receives.

Vital checks

A major drawback of do-it-yourself servicing in the home garage is the tendency of most owners to ignore the underside of the car: a case of out of sight, out of mind, perhaps?

Don't be tempted to crawl under the car when it is supported only by a jack or by a pile of bricks, however. A pair of drive-on wheel ramps will usually give enough clearance, or the car can be taken to your neighbourhood dealer at least twice a year to be put on a lift or over a pit so that the whole of the underside can be thoroughly inspected at leisure. It is well worthwhile to pay for this service, if necessary, or to hire a self-service bay if a garage is operating this scheme in your district.

If the underside is coated with mud and filth, it will obviously pay to hose it down thoroughly, or better still, to have it steam-cleaned, before starting work. Garages which service commercial vehicles usually have steam-cleaning equipment, but the cost of the work, although well worthwhile, is not cheap.

Now for the vital check points:

First go over the whole of the underside of the car for any signs of flaking paint, peeling underbody coating, if this has been applied, and the beginning of rust. Pay particular attention to the sub-frames and the areas around the suspension mountings.

Check the brake pipes inch by inch for any signs of chafing, rust or pitting. A small corrosion pit can eat through a new pipe within two years, causing a pin-hole leak which may result in complete loss of brake fluid.

Check the flexible brake hoses for perishing. chafing and leakage from the unions.

There will probably have been some oil leakage from the engine and transmission units, but a heavy leak obviously calls for investigation.

Examine the inner walls of the tyres for cuts or splits. It is surprising how often accidental damage occurs on the inside wall of a tyre, rather than on the outside, where it would be immediately visible. While checking the tyres, look for any signs of rubbing against the body when the springs are fully compressed or when the front wheels are turned to full lock.

Check the exhaust system for rust, damage and leakage and make sure that the supports are sound.

Finally, push, pull and shake all suspension and steering components vigorously, to show up any wear or loose attachments.

1 Engine tie-rod
2 Heater water tap
3 Engine oil filler
4 Oil-bath air cleaner
5 Fume-extractor hose
6 Carburettor
7 Bonnet safety catch
8 Radiator filler cap
9 Sparking plugs
10 Ignition coil
11 Ignition distributor (oil dipstick beside distributor)

Fig. 4.1 This underbonnet view of a typical Minor 1000 shows some of the main routine servicing points

Maintenance summary

This chart has been arranged to show at a glance the frequency with which the various jobs must be done. The items which make up a complete service can thus be identified and the work spread over several week-ends, if necessary. Remember that the columns are cumulative: the 3 000 mile jobs must be repeated at 6000 and 9000 miles, the 6000 mile service at 12 000 miles (plus the jobs in the 12 000 mile column), and so on

Vital safety checks

	Weekly or before a long journey	Every 3000 miles (5000 km) or 3 months	Every 6000 miles (10 000 km) or 6 months	Every 12 000 miles (20 000 km) or 12 months	Every 24 000 miles (40 000 km) or 2 years
Wheels and Tyres Check tyre pressures when cold. Watch for signs of uneven wear. Check tightness of wheel nuts	●				
Brake Fluid Reservoir Check level of fluid (this is a precautionary check only — topping-up should be required only at long intervals, unless a leak has developed in system)	●				
Brakes Check pedal travel; adjust brakes if necessary. Inspect brake pipes and hoses for leakage		●			
Brakes — Preventive Check Check thickness of linings. Check operating cylinders for leakage. Clean out dust. Check handbrake adjustment. Check pipes and flexible hoses for chafing. Renew all flexible hoses and rubber seals in braking system after 40 000 miles (65 000 km) or 3 years in service. Change fluid after 2 years in service. Some authorities recommend a yearly change			●		
Wheels Remove road wheels, wash and examine for possible damage			●		
Exhaust System Check for corrosion, leakage and security of attachments			●		
Lighting System Check headlamp beam alignment, lamp glasses for cracks, side, tail and indicator lamps for blackened bulbs, rusty contacts and water in lampholders		●			

Lubrication

	Weekly or before a long journey	Every 3000 miles (5000 km) or 3 months	Every 6000 miles (10 000 km) or 6 months	Every 12 000 miles (20 000 km) or 12 months	Every 24 000 miles (40 000 km) or 2 years
Engine Check oil-level and top-up if necessary (check daily if engine is worn and also when refilling with fuel on long run)	●				
Engine Drain oil and re-fill sump. Renew oil-filter element			●		
Ignition Distributor Lubricate			●		
Dynamo Lubricate end bearing			●		
Gearbox Check oil level			●		
Rear axle Check oil level			●		
Water pump Lubricate sparingly with grease				●	
Clutch Lubricate pedal shaft and linkage			●		
Grease-gun Lubrication Lubricate all grease nipples — except steering rack and pinion		●			
Steering Rack and Pinion Lubricate with grease-gun filled with gear oil				●	
Semaphore-type Direction Indicators Lubricate pivots sparingly with thin oil			●		
Oil-can Lubrication Apply a few drops of oil to throttle linkage, handbrake linkage, door, boot and bonnet locks and hinges			●		
Speedometer Cable Lubricate inner cable with grease					●

Servicing and adjustments

- **Radiator** Check water-level and top-up if necessary
- **Cooling System** Check condition of hoses, and for leaks. Check tension of fan/generator driving belt
- **Cooling System** De-scale, flush and refill. Check operation of thermostat (this should be a regular autumn service)
- **Battery** Check level of liquid in cells
- **Windscreen Washer Reservoir** Check level of fluid. Add special anti-freeze solvent in winter (*not* radiator anti-freeze)
- **Engine** Check valve tappet clearances. Adjust if necessary
- **Carburettor** Top-up piston damper with oil. Check damper piston for freedom. Check slow-running adjustments
- **Carburettor Air-cleaner** Clean filter or fit new pleated-paper element
- **Carburettor** Clean float chamber, piston and suction chamber
- **Fuel Pump** Check pump and clean contact points and filter if necessary.
- **Sparking Plugs** Clean; check gaps and re-set if necessary
- **Ignition System** Fit new sparking plugs and new contact-breaker points. Preferably do this at 10 000 miles (16 000 km)
- **Ignition Distributor** Clean or renew contact points and adjust gap. Clean distributor rotor and cap. Check timing. Preferably have system checked with electronic test-tune equipment
- **Clutch** Check free movement of pedal and if necessary adjust
- **Steering and Front Suspension** Check bellows on rack-and-pinion unit for splits or leakage. Check steering and suspension joints for damaged grease-retaining gaiters and wear.
- **Steering and Front Suspension** Have front wheel alignment and steering geometry checked with special equipment
- **Front Wheel Bearings** Check for leakage of grease, excessive end-play and noise when wheel is rotated
- **Wheels** Change from side to side at front and rear. Grease wheel studs. Have wheel balance checked
- **Braking System** Drain brake fluid from system, flush, refill and bleed-off air. This should be done every 2 years if mileage is less than 24 000 miles (40 000 km) in this period
- **Electrical System** Clean and tighten battery terminals. Check operation of charging system, starter motor, lights and instruments
- **Dynamo** Check condition of brushes and commutator
- **Starter Motor** Check condition of brushes, commutator and pinion drive assembly
- **Road Test** Give car a thorough road test and carry out any adjustments required. If possible, have final check made with electronic test-tune equipment and check all plugs, flanges, joints and unions

Your basic tool kit

The items below will be needed for routine servicing. More specialized tools can be added, as necessary, when repairs and overhauls are undertaken and a list of these is given at the beginning of each workshop manual section.

Special service tools tend to be rather expensive, but you may be able to hire them from your local British Leyland dealer. The most frequently needed items, such as extractors, however, can usually be purchased from car accessory shops and these are usually cheaper than the 'official' service tools. Alternatively, there may be a shop in your neighbourhood which hires-out tools at reasonable charges.

A basic tool kit for routine servicing and minor repairs should include —

Set of open-ended or ring, or combination spanners (A/F sizes)
Set of socket spanners, with extensions and
  preferably a universal joint
Selection of screwdrivers, including two sizes
  for cross-head screws
Large and small adjustable spanners
Self-locking adjustable spanner (Mole wrench type)
Side-cutting and pointed-nose 6 in. pliers
Set of feeler gauges
Sparking plug gap-setting tool
Tyre tread-depth gauge
Engineer's hammer (ball pane)
Soft-faced hammer (with hide, plastic or
  copper faces)
Fine carborundum stone
Wire brush
Inspection lamp

A good tyre-pressure gauge is essential. Garage pressure gauges are not always as accurate as they should be; and pressures should always be checked with the tyres *cold,* which is obviously impossible if the car has to be driven to a garage or if pressures are checked during the course of a journey.

A tread-depth gauge is an inexpensive item which will enable you to keep a check on the rate of wear of the tyres and will also indicate when they are due for replacement. The official regulation in Britain calls for 1 mm of tread over three-quarters of the width of the tread pattern, around the complete circumference of the tyre, but it is much safer to change the tyres when the treads are worn down to a depth of 2 mm.

An electrical drill is, perhaps, something of a luxury, but the way in which it can speed-up a surprisingly large number of jobs, particularly if it is provided with the usual range of accessories, such as wire brushes for decarbonizing the cylinder head, a grindstone and a lambswool polishing mop, renders it a really worthwhile investment for an owner who carries out any appreciable amount of work.

Preserving the woodwork on the Traveller

It is important not to allow the ash framework for the bodywork of the Traveller to deteriorate, since the wooden members are not merely decorative — they form part of the structure of the body, to which the metal panels are attached. If the varnish is neglected and rot sets in, renewing them can be an expensive and time-consuming job.

When replacements are not readily available from a Leyland dealer, you may be able to make up new components yourself. In any case the work should be within the scope of a competent carpenter. An epoxy resin glue should be used for the mortise-and-tenon joints.

Prevention is better than cure, however, and trouble should not be experienced if the woodwork is rubbed down once a year and refinished with at least two coats of marine varnish, preferably of the polyurethane type.

Stained patches can be bleached by using an oxalic acid solution. A chemist will be able to supply the acid, but remember that it is poisonous. The bleaching should be followed by thorough washing, before sanding and varnishing.

Be careful not to block the various drain holes when applying the varnish. If water is allowed to lie on the side rails, the risk of rot setting in is greatly increased.

Workbench and vice

A workbench will be needed for any jobs that are done on components that have been removed from the car, but it is quite possible to make do with a stout kitchen table, which can often be picked up cheaply at an auction. If any but elementary servicing is carried out, a vice will be needed. This can often be obtained quite cheaply from a surplus equipment shop.

Working beneath the car

If an inspection pit is not available, a pair of drive-on wheel ramps will also be needed, or a pair of adjustable axle stands. These have the advantage of leaving the wheels free to rotate and are more useful than ramps when carrying out overhauls. On the other hand, when servicing it takes only a minute or two to drive the front or rear wheels on to a pair of ramps, whereas both sides of the car must be jacked-up to allow stands to be placed below the jacking points.

For obvious reaons, ramps or axle-stands which lift only one end of the car must not be used when checking the oil-levels.

Finally, never be tempted to work beneath the car when it is supported only by the jack or by an insecure pile of bricks.

Part two

5 Trouble-shooting
Systematic diagnosis

The risk of an unexpected breakdown must obviously be greatly reduced by regular servicing. The work described in Chapter 4 can therefore be described as *preventive* maintenance in the best sense of the word; it aims at detecting or forestalling trouble before it becomes serious. Most faults, in fact, can be traced back to neglect at some stage. Dirt, lack of lubrication or incorrect adjustment are the most frequent culprits.

When devising the special trouble-shooting charts in this section, we had in mind mainly the practical owner, who often has to trace a fault without the benefit of a voltmeter, an ammeter, a vacuum gauge, a cylinder compression-pressure gauge or a simple stethoscope. These useful aids to diagnosis are usually conspicuous by their absence when the car breaks down miles from the home base!

The aim has been to produce a set of charts which will encourage a logical process of elimination. Inspired guesswork (intelligent intuition?) will sometimes get results, but systematic investigation will usually be less time-consuming in tracking-down obscure faults — although there are, of course, occasions on which the possibility of a particular fault can be assumed with a fair amount of certainty.

Take the case of a normally well-behaved engine that refuses to fire from cold after the car has been parked in the open during a spell of damp, misty weather, for example. Condensation on the high-tension leads, ignition coil, distributor, and sparking-plug insulators is almost a certainty, and a spray with one of the water-repelling aerosol fluids, or a wipe with a dry cloth, will usually be all that is needed to restore normal starting.

Similarly, if an engine runs well, but is a brute to start from cold, suspect too weak a starting mixture. Make sure that the mixture control is operating properly and that the petrol pump is delivering plenty of fuel. If the engine is reluctant to start when hot, on the other hand, check for an over-rich mixture. In either case, if the carburation seems to be satisfactory, the ignition system should be checked-over, following the step-by-step charts in this chapter.

Now a word as to how to use the trouble-tracing charts.

By reading vertically down the column, under the various symptoms, the most likely causes of the trouble can be picked out and eliminated one by one. Alternatively, by reading horizontally across the chart, a combination of different symptoms will often point pretty conclusively to one particular fault which is causing the trouble.

In some cases, these charts cover alternative types of equipment. To find out which items apply to your model, consult the Specifications and Overhaul Data at the end of this book.

Preventing trouble and restoring performance

There is a great deal to be said for carrying out a systematic inspection of the car at regular intervals — say, every 5000-6000 miles — in order to detect any incipient trouble and to correct any faults which may exist.

A ten-point check and tune-up to restore engine efficiency is outlined on page 19. A suggested routine for a more thorough check of the whole car is given in the fault-tracing and condition report sheet. If these checks are conscientiously carried out and any necessary adjustments are made, they will restore 'new car' performance on a vehicle that is in reasonably good mechanical condition. Any major faults which are present, such as loss of engine compression, and transmission or similar troubles, will, of course, require attention as soon as possible.

An inspection record of this type has, in itself, a number of advantages. Not only does it ensure that no item is overlooked, but it also enables the general condition of the car to be assessed at a glance. If completed systematically at each inspection period and filed for reference purposes, it will serve as a guide to the reconditioning required and as a check on the performance of each item.

When made out for the first time, as with a newly-purchased used car, the chart is almost certain to reveal defects that might otherwise have been unsuspected and that might have developed into major troubles.

Inspection record

Vehicle make and year_____
Capacity or horse power_____
Reg. number _____
Speedometer reading_____
Date of inspection _____

Engine and accessories

Compression

Tappets: clearance; noise

Valve gear: noise; cover gaskets

Timing gears or chain: noise; backlash

Cylinder head: nuts; gaskets

Manifolds: securing nuts; gaskets; air or gas leaks

Driving belts: fan; dynamo; accessories

Water pump: leakage; effectiveness

Radiator: water level; leakage; filler cap; condition of core; shutters; relief valve; overflow pipe

Oil leaks: crankcase; pipes and unions; timing covers; main bearings; drain plugs

Oil filters

Engine mountings

Carburettor and fuel pump

Jets

Float chamber level

Cold starting device: interconnecting linkage thermostat; dashboard control

Fuel pump: effectiveness; delivery pressure

Filters: carburettor; petrol pump; air cleaner

Ignition system

Contact breaker points: gap; condition

Rotor: condition

Distributor cap: cleanliness; cracks; tracking

Timing control: manual; centrifugal; suction operated

Coil and wiring: efficiency; condition of high and low tension wiring; support

Sparking plugs: gap at points; condition of points and insulators; washers

Electrical system

Dynamo or alternator: charging rate

Dynamo brushes and commutator: burning or pitting; chatter and sparking

Dynamo or alternator drive: condition of belt, tension

Voltage regulator

Ammeter: accuracy

Battery: acid level; specific gravity; voltage of each cell; connections; corrosion

Lights

Headlamps: focus and alignment; condition of reflectors

Side lamps

Tail lamps

Stop lamp

Other lamps: ignition warning; interior; trafficators

Switches and fuses

Electrical accessories

Windscreen wipers: efficiency; noise; condition of blades

Indicators

Starter: efficiency; condition of pinion and fly-wheel teeth

Horns

Interior heater

Defroster

Radio

Steering

Lost motion

Stiffness

Front axle alignment: toe-in; castor and camber angles

Swivels and bushes

Front hub bearings

Steering linkage and joints

Suspension

Springs: condition

Shock absorbers: effectiveness; fluid leaks; security of attachments

Torque reaction rods or cables: adjustment; security of attachment

Brakes

Pedal travel

Condition of rods or cables

Hydraulic system: fluid level; leakage from pipe lines, choked pipes, air in system

Handbrake: adjustment; condition of ratchet

Servo mechanism: vacuum servo; pipe lines

Bodywork

General appearance

Windows: winding controls; glass; channels

Doors: alignment; buffers; locks; check straps

Sunshine roof: operation; water leaks

Seats: condition of springs; adjustments

Bumpers: condition; attachments

Tool kit

Fire extinguisher, safety belts

Transmission

Clutch: adjustment

Backlash: in universal joints; in back axle; in gearbox

Rear axle: leakage

Wheels

Rims: buckling; rust

Wheel nuts: tightness; condition of studs; splines on knock-off wheels

Tyres

Pressures

Tread wear

Condition of sidewalls

Valves and caps

Road test

Engine	Clutch	Gearbox	Suspension	Back axle
Ease of starting	Slip	Noisy gears	Comfort	Noise on drive
Oil pressure when hot	Fierceness	Synchromesh operation	Roll on corners	Noise on overrun
Idling	Spinning	Preselector operation		Noise on corners
Acceleration	Unusual noises	Vibration on gear lever	**Brakes**	
Maximum speed		Gears jumping out of mesh	Power	**Steering**
Fuel consumption	**Propeller shaft**		Balance	Positiveness
Oil consumption	Vibration	**Instruments**	Smoothness	Castor action
Engine temperature	Noise	Functioning	Judder or squeal	Wander
Exhaust: noise, restriction; smoke		Accuracy	Binding	Road shocks at steering wheel
General noise, fumes				

Ten-point engine check and tune-up

The ten-point check on engine efficiency described in this section carries the principle of preventive maintenance, already outlined in Part 1, a stage further.

The object of an engine tune-up at an intermediate stage is to check deterioration: to restore the keen edge of engine efficiency, with a bonus in the form of improved performance and better fuel consumption. A good time to carry it out would be between the 5000-6000 miles services.

1 Electrical check

The effectiveness of the ignition system depends on sound electrical connections throughout the low-tension and high-tension wiring. Check them systematically, starting at the battery terminals and the earthing strap, and working via the ignition switch to the low-tension terminals on the ignition coil, and from there to the terminal on the side of the ignition distributor.

Check the security of the high-tension leads in the distributor cap and coil by lightly tugging them. Bear in mind that modern carbon-trace ignition cables usually have a. life of about two years. After that, misfiring is increasingly likely. A new set of leads will often rejuvenate an engine.

2 Check carburettor and manifold flange nuts

The nuts must not be loose but must never be overtightened—particularly the carburettor flange nuts—owing to the risk of distorting or cracking the flanges, a fault which is a common cause of air leakage into the induction system, resulting in a weak mixture, misfiring and difficult starting.

3 Clean the carburettor filter (when fitted) and the float chamber

Traces of sediment or water in the float chamber can upset the carburation and cause misfiring.

4 Fuel pump check

If the fuel pump does not deliver its maximum output when the engine is operating under full-throttle, continuous high-speed conditions, fuel starvation may cause severe exhaust-valve burning and possibly piston failure. If in doubt, have the pump checked by a garage, using a special flow-test rig.

5 Check the ignition distributor and contact-breaker

Peak efficiency cannot be expected if the contact-breaker points are dirty, badly pitted or incorrectly gapped. Distributor checks are covered in the section dealing with the ignition system.

6 Check the ignition timing

Again refer to the section dealing with the ignition system. The correct ignition timing is critical, affecting both performance and fuel consumption.

7 Remove and check the sparking plugs

The plugs are a good guide to running conditions, as shown by the colour illustrations in this chapter. Clean them if necessary and re-set the gaps. Carry out a compression check (below) before refitting them.

8 Compression test

The compression check gives a reliable indication of the efficiency of the valves, piston rings and cylinder bores. A compression gauge is not expensive. The simple type which combines a compression gauge with a tyre-pressure gauge will give reliable readings.

Bring the engine to normal running temperature. Remove all the sparking plugs and wedge or tie the throttle fully open. The compressions should be recorded at normal cranking speed which must remain constant throughout the test, so the battery must be well charged.

Make a note of the number of pulsations required to obtain a maximum gauge reading for the first cylinder tested. The same number of crankshaft revs should be used when testing the other cylinders.

When the first set of readings has been recorded, repeat the tests with approximately a tablespoonful of engine oil injected into each cylinder. Higher readings may now be obtained on some or all of the cylinders, indicating that the oil has sealed any leakage past the piston rings that was occurring during the first tests.

Any remaining differences between the maximum pressures recorded for the individual cylinder which exceed about 10lb per sq. in. are probably due to leakage past the valves (possibly due to wrong valve clearances). It is also possible that the cylinder head gasket is leaking, but this would normally cause overheating and, in some case, misfiring.

9 Check carburettor idling adjustments

Refit the plugs and adjust the carburettor idling speed and mixture strength. These adjustments are fully described in the chapter dealing with the carburettor and fuel system.

10 Road test

Carry out a thorough road test as described in the section which deals with vetting a used car. Record the figures and file them for reference when the next tune-up is carried out. 'Before and after' comparisons will then quickly show up any loss of efficiency and indicate the need for further action.

At-a-glance trouble-shooting chart 1
Engine faults - key chart

Symptoms

System	Engine will not start	Starts but will not keep running	Stalls during normal running	Poor idling	Misfiring at all speeds	Not giving full power or revs	Fuel consumption excessive	Oil consumption excessive	Pinking or detonation	Overheating, pre-ignition, running-on	Unusual noises
Carburation and Fuel System Chart 5	●	●	●	●	●	●	●		●	●	
Ignition System Chart 4	●	●	●	●	●	●	●		●	●	
Electrical System Chart 10	●										
Mechanical Faults Chart 2	●	●	●	●	●	●	●	●	●	●	●
Cooling System Chart 3						●	●	●	●	●	

First - Check your plugs

Normal
Nose lightly coated with grey brown deposits. Electrodes not burning unduly — gap increasing about .001 in. per 1000 miles. Plugs ideally suited to engine.

Carbon fouling
Deposits can short circuit the firing end. If recommended plug is fitted check for over-rich mixture, faulty choke mechanism or clogged air cleaner.

Oil fouling
Deposits can short circuit the firing end and this weakens or eliminates the spark. May be caused by worn valve guides, bores or piston rings or by running in an overhauled engine.

Overheating
Likely causes are overadvanced ignition timing, wrong grade of plug, use of too low octane fuel, weak mixture, or cooling system troubles.

At-a-glance trouble-shooting chart 2

Engine: mechanical faults and noise

Running conditions and probable causes	Tapping or clicking — Cylinder head or block	Knock, tapping or light clatter — Cylinder head or top of block	Clatter or knocking — Crankcase or front of engine	Light clatter or chattering — Cylinder head	High-pitched metallic tapping — Audible when accelerating	Scraping noise — Cylinder block	Knocking, rumbling or thumping — Crankcase	Lashing, rattling or grinding noise — Timing chain cover	Squeaks or whistles — Front of engine or near manifolds
Engine cold—worn pistons, rings, cylinder bores (piston slap)[1]		●							
Engine hot—worn little-end bearings[1]		●							
Engine hot, more evident when idling—worn camshaft bearings			●						
Valve-rocker clearances too great, worn valve-operating mechanism, bent push-rod	●			●					
Broken piston rings[2]	●					●			
Engine under load or when revved in neutral—big-end bearing wear[3]			●						
Engine under load and hot—'pinking' caused by pre-ignition or detonation[4]					●				
Crankcase, engine under load—main-bearing and/or crankshaft journal wear[3]							●		
Loose flywheel							●		
Occurring at high revs—valve-bounce (possibly weak valve springs)				●					
Loose or broken engine mounting							●		
Worn timing chain (when fitted).								●	
Defective chain tensioner									
Front of engine—loose crankshaft pulley or worn pulley key (can be mistaken for big-end bearing wear)			●						
Front of engine—worn, glazed or slipping fan belt. Worn or dry generator or fan bearings. Noisy water pump bearing or seal									●
Vicinity of inlet and exhaust manifolds—loose manifold bolts or nuts, or defective gaskets									●

1 Noise can be reduced or eliminated by shorting-out appropriate sparking plug

2 Badly-worn rings and grooves in pistons may also cause clicking

3 Usually accompanied by low oil pressure

4 Check that correct grade of fuel is in use. Also see Chart 1

At-a-glance trouble-shooting chart 3
Cooling system

This is a general chart covering water-cooled and air-cooled engines. All the items apply to water-cooled systems but only those marked with an asterisk affect air-cooled engines

Symptoms

Probable causes	*Overheating at normal atmospheric temperatures	*Overheating in very cold weather	*Engine slow to warm-up	*Engine does not reach normal running temperature	*Radiator needs frequent topping-up
* Fan belt – not correctly tensioned or broken	●				
Radiator filler cap – not sealing properly, or wrong pressure rating	●				●
Thermostat – faulty or wrong rating	●		●	●	
* Radiator or cooling fins – water or air passages clogged	●				
Water passages in cylinder head or block – choked by deposits of lime, rust or sludge	●				
Radiator – frozen at base (no anti-freeze, or too low a concentration)		●			
Water pump – inefficient or inoperative	●				
Air-lock – in cooling system or heater	●				●
Water hoses – leaking (check with engine revved-up)					●
Water hoses – perished, collapsed or obstructed by disintegrated linings	●				
Internal water or gas leakage – caused by faulty cylinder-head gasket, cracked head or cylinder block	●				●
Local boiling in cylinder head – rust and lime deposits, filler cap pressure rating too low, or cap leaking	●				●
* Ignition faults – retarded timing, pre-ignition or detonation (see Chart 4)	●				
* Carburation – faults causing weak mixture (see Chart 5)	●				
* Brakes – binding (see Chart 9)	●				
* Exhaust system – choked or damaged, restricting flow of gas	●				
* Engine – assembled too tightly after overhaul	●				

At-a-glance trouble-shooting chart 4
Ignition system faults

The faults in this chart are confined to the ignition system. Some of the symptoms may be caused by carburation, mechanical or cooling system faults. These are dealt with in Charts 2, 3, 5

Engine running symptoms

Probable causes	Engine will not start	Starts but will not keep running	Stalls during normal running	Poor idling	Mis-firing at all speeds	Mis-firing at high speed	Not giving full power or revs	Fuel consumption excessive	Pinking or detonation	Overheating, pre-ignition, running-on
Battery voltage too low – discharged or defective battery, resulting in heavy 'coil robbing' due to current drain by starter	•									
Cold-start coil circuit (when fitted) defective	•	•								
Low-tension circuit – faulty ignition switch, loose connections, faulty earthing strap (engine or battery to frame)	•	•	•	•	•	•	•	•		
Sparking plugs – wrong gap, dirty or worn-out	•	•		•	•	•	•	•	•	•
Sparking plugs – wrong type fitted				•	•	•	•		•	•
Contact-breaker points – dirty or pitted, wrong gap, incorrectly assembled, sticking open	•	•		•	•	•	•	•	•	•
Contact-breaker – weak contact spring				•	•	•	•	•		
Contact-breaker – broken spring	•									
High-tension circuit – current leakage across coil, distributor cap or rotor: insulation cracked, dirty or damp	•	•	•	•	•	•	•	•		
High-tension leads – poor contact at terminals, breaks in internal conductors, leads shorting to earth or to each other, faulty suppressors (when fitted)	•	•	•	•	•	•	•	•		
Sparking plug leads – connected in wrong sequence	•			•	•	•	•			
High-tension polarity incorrect – ignition to coil low tension connections reversed		•		•	•	•	•	•		
Distributor cap centre contact broken or sticking		•	•	•	•	•	•	•		
Coil or condenser – open-circuit, short-circuit, intermittent faults	•	•	•	•	•	•	•	•		
Static ignition timing – incorrect	•	•	•	•	•	•	•	•	•	•
Centrifugal timing mechanism – not functioning correctly				•	•	•	•	•	•	
Vacuum timing mechanism – not functioning correctly				•	•	•	•	•	•	
Distributor – shaft bearing worn			•	•	•	•	•	•	•	
Distributor – wrong type fitted	•			•	•	•	•	•	•	•

At-a-glance trouble-shooting chart 5

Carburettor and fuel system

The faults in this chart are confined to the carburettor and fuel system. Some of the symptoms may be caused by other faults, which are dealt with in Charts 2, 3, 4.

Symptoms

Probable causes	Engine will not start	Starts but will not keep running	Stalls during normal running	Poor idling	Misfiring at all speeds	Not giving full power or revs	Fuel consumption excessive	Pinking or detonation	Overheating, pre-ignition, running-on
Carburettor(s)									
No petrol in float chamber – petrol tank empty, float needle valve sticking faulty fuel pump, filter clogged, petrol pipe obstructed, pipe union loose (see *Petrol Pump, Pipes and Tank*)	●								
Mixture (choke) control not lowering jet fully (S.U. carburettor)	●	●							
Mixture (choke) control not returning to 'off' position		●		●	●		●		
Hydraulic damper needs topping-up (S.U. carburettor)				●	●	●			
Carburettor suction piston sticking (S.U. carburettor). Choked jets (Zenith, Solex, Weber carburettors)	●	●		●	●	●	●	●	●
Carburettor flooding – float needle valve not seating, fuel pump pressure too high	●	●		●	●	●	●		
Air leakage past carburettor or manifold flanges								●	●
Water or sediment in float chamber		●	●	●	●	●			●
Idling speed and mixture adjustments incorrect				●	●	●			
Twin carburettors not properly synchronized						●	●		●
Wrong jet needle, jet or piston spring fitted (S.U. and Stromberg carburettors). Wrong size of jet, faulty acceleration pump (Zenith, Solex, Weber carburettors)	●	●			●	●		●	●
Carburettor icing-up internally (normal running restored when carburettor warms-up). See also *Air Cleaner*			●						
Petrol pump, pipes and tank									
Electric pump – dirty filter, poor electrical connections, dirty contacts	●	●	●		●	●		●	●
Mechanical pump – dirty filter, air leak at filter cover flange	●	●	●		●	●		●	●
Electrical or mechanical pump – delivery pressure excessive	●					●	●		
Fuel pipes – clogged, loose unions, vapour-lock in fuel pipe	●	●	●	●	●	●			
Petrol tank – empty (fuel gauge may be giving wrong reading)	●	●	●	●	●	●			
Petrol tank – air-vent obstructed, internal filter clogged	●	●	●		●	●			
Air cleaner									
Filter clogged, overdue for renewal						●	●		●
Air intake not correctly positioned for summer or winter use or thermostatically-controlled flap not functioning properly (may cause carburettor icing in winter – see *Carburettor icing-up*)						●	●		

At-a-glance trouble-shooting chart 6
Clutch and transmission

This chart deals only with manual transmissions. Automatic transmission torque converters and gearboxes are complex units and special test equipment, which is held by authorized dealers, must be used to diagnose faults in them

Probable causes	Clutch slip	Clutch judder or snatch	Rattle, knock or squeal from clutch	Difficulty in engaging gear	Jumping out of gear	Noisy gearbox	Rattle or buzz from gear lever	Rattle from transmission when idling	Knocking or clicking from front of car when cornering
Air in clutch hydraulic operating system – needs bleeding (hydraulically-operated clutches)				●					
Clutch adjustment incorrect	●			●					
Clutch driven plate – worn, or oil on friction lining	●								
Clutch release bearing dry and due for renewal			●						
Clutch driven plate buckled during assembly		●							
Clutch release mechanism worn			●	●					
Clutch hub splines worn		●	●						
Gears and/or bearings worn					●	●		●	
Gear teeth chipped						●			
Selector linkage worn or damaged				●	●		●		
Gear lever pivot and linkage worn or needs lubrication							●		
Synchromesh mechanism worn				●	●				
Noise caused by transfer-gears on some front-wheel drive models – difficult to cure at idling speed, but careful carburettor adjustment helps								●	
Universal joints at outer ends of driving shafts worn and due for renewal (front-wheel drive cars only)									●

At-a-glance trouble-shooting chart 7

Suspension

This is a general trouble-shooting chart, applicable to most suspension systems using leaf springs, coil springs, torsion bars and also hydro-pneumatic systems (eg British Leyland Hydrolastics, Hydragas and other pressurized systems using gas and hydraulic fluid)

Symptoms

Probable causes	'Bouncy' ride — insufficient damping	Car too low at front and/or rear	Car sags to one side	Groaning or grunting from suspension	Squeak from front or rear suspension	Knock from front suspension	Knock from rear suspension	Rumble or whine from front or rear suspension
Weak or broken springs. Incorrect pressure in hydro-pneumatic system or loss of fluid	●	●	●					
Weak springs allowing suspension to hit bump stops						●	●	
Noisy damper valves in hydro-pneumatic system				●				
Broken check strap							●	
Faulty shock absorbers or hydro-pneumatic unit	●							
Worn shock absorber bushes or loose mountings						●	●	
Squeak from rubber components – to cure, spray with silicone fluid or brush on brake fluid (not mineral oil)					●			
Worn bushes in radius arms or links						●	●	
Worn bushes in tie-bars, suspension arms or linkage					●	●	●	
Worn or incorrectly adjusted wheel bearings								
Worn, unlubricated or incorrectly adjusted wheel bearings								●

At-a-glance trouble-shooting chart 8

Steering and controlability

Symptoms

Probable causes	Excessive free movement at steering wheel	Car wanders, or 'oversteers' excessively	Car pulls to one side	Heavy steering	Wheel wobble or vibration at steering wheel	Rattle or knock from beneath front floor near passenger's feet	Knock from base of steering column
Incorrect tyre pressures		●	●	●	●		
Rear tyre pressures too low		●					
Incorrect steering geometry and/or front-wheel alignment		●	●		●		
Tyres 'out of round,' or unbalanced tyres and wheels – have front and rear wheels balanced regularly					●		
Worn or incorrectly adjusted steering and suspension joints and/or wheel hub bearings	●		●		●		
Worn or incorrectly adjusted steering rack-and-pinion	●		●	●			
Distortion of column or rack-and-pinion unit caused by incorrect fitting				●			
Loose bolts holding rack-and-pinion unit to bulkhead	●				●	●	
Loose clamping bolt on steering column clamp or universal joint	●				●		●
Worn bush in rack-and-pinion unit						●	
Lack of oil in rack-and-pinion unit – check condition of telescopic gaiters				●		●	
Accidental damage – have suspension and steering units checked by authorized dealer			●	●			
Braking system faults – brakes unevenly adjusted, faulty hydraulic system, oil or grease on linings, brake discs running out-of-true. See Chart 9			●		●		
Suspension faults causing insufficient damping, sagging to one side or incorrect suspension height at front or rear – see Chart 7			●				

At-a-glance trouble-shooting chart 9
Braking system

This chart covers the most common faults in the full range of braking systems – all-drum, disc-and-drum and servo-assisted installations. When disc brakes or a servo are not fitted, the relevant items in the chart do not, of course, apply

Symptoms

Probable causes	Excessive pedal travel	Pedal feels spongy	Brakes lack power	Brakes bind or fail to release fully	Unbalanced braking – locking or pulling to one side	Brake judder	Brake squeal	Rapid wear of linings
Brakes incorrectly adjusted	●		●	●	●			●
Fluid level in reservoir too low		●	●					
Rubber seals in hydraulic cylinders swollen		●	●	●	●			●
Wheel cylinder or caliper piston seized	●		●	●	●			●
Leakage past seals in main or wheel cylinders, or from pipeline	●	●	●		●			
Internal fluid leak in servo (level in reservoir falls without visible external leak)		●	●					
Accumulation of brake dust in drums			●				●	
Badly-scored discs or drums			●		●	●	●	●
Worn wheel bearings	●				●	●	●	
Wrong type of friction linings fitted	●		●			●	●	●
Brakes 'fading' due to excessive use or wrong grade of linings	●		●					
Brake fluid boiling in wheel cylinders – pump all fluid out of system, refill with correct fluid and bleed brakes			●					
Master-cylinder, wheel cylinder or caliper bolts loose			●		●	●	●	
Air in system – requires bleeding		●	●					
New linings or pads not bedded-in		●	●					
Disc running out of true or drums distorted					●	●		
Water, oil or brake fluid on linings			●		●	●	●	
Servo defective	●		●	●				
Servo vacuum hose leaking or non-return valve faulty			●					
Pedal push-rod incorrectly adjusted				●				●
Handbrake operating levers or cable guides seized with rust or mud – brakes remain on or partly applied				●				●
Faulty rear-brake pressure-regulating valve					●			
Worn steering and suspension parts – see Charts 7 and 8					●	●		

At-a-glance trouble-shooting chart   10

Electrical equipment

It has been possible to deal only with the broader aspects of electrical fault-tracing in this chart. Detailed diagnosis calls for the use of accurate instruments and a good deal of electrical know-how. It is best left to a qualified auto-electrician

Symptoms

Probable causes	Battery and Charging system				Starter motor		Lamps			
	Battery cells need frequent topping-up with water	Battery apparently not receiving sufficient charge	Battery will not hold charge	Starter does not turn engine, or rotates it slowly	Starter runs but pinion does not engage with flywheel gear	Starter pinion jams in mesh of flywheel gear	Headlamps give poor illumination when correctly aligned	Brightness of lights varies noticeably with engine speed	Lights flicker	Bulbs or light units burn out frequently
Battery discharged				•			•	•		
Battery electrolyte level too low or of wrong specific gravity		•	•							
Defective battery — sulphated or buckled plates		•	•	•			•	•		
Generator driving belt slipping		•						•		
Faulty generator		•						•		
Charging regulator defective or incorrectly adjusted. Charging rate too high or too low	•	•						•		•
Loose or high-resistance connections in charging circuit		•						•		•
Loose or high-resistance connections in lighting circuits							•		•	
Corroded or loose battery terminals		•		•				•	•	•
Poor earth-return connections				•			•		•	
Leakage of current in car wiring			•							
Faulty starter switch				•						
Poor connections in starter circuit				•	•					
Dirty or faulty starter pinion drive					•	•				
Worn starter pinion teeth on flywheel ring gear						•				
Faulty starter motor				•						

6 Bodywork Defects
Dealing with dents, scratches and rust

One of the recurring themes in this book is 'Prevention is better than cure'. In Chapter 3 we emphasize the importance of making a careful check for rust. Here we are concerned with minimizing its effects. Neglect even a minor blemish, and you will find that rust can spread with alarming rapidity under the surrounding paintwork.

1 Dealing with scratches and chips

As shown in the first photograph, it is best to use a fine brush for touching-in small blemishes. If an aerosol paint spray is used it is difficult to confine the spray to a very small area. We give some notes on spraying larger areas at the end of this section.

Scrape any loose paint and rust from the area with the tip of a penknife blade, apply a rust-preventive, such as Zinc Plate, to the bright metal and then knife-on a thin layer of cellulose stopping, building up the level to slightly above the surrounding paintwork.

When the stopping is dry, rub it down with very fine wet-or-dry paper, used wet; with a smear of soap to prevent clogging. Then touch-in the area with the correct colour to match the surrounding finish.

Alternatively, your accessory shop may sell a card of special paint transfers which, when applied on a clean surface and rubbed down, produce an almost indetectable repair to a scratch or chip.

2 Removing dents

The second picture shows the sort of dent that can be dealt with at home by filling it with glass-fibre resin paste.

Rub down to bare metal, extending to about 2 in. beyond the edge of the dent, using 80 grit paper. Score the base and sides of the dent with a file or screwdriver to provide a key for the body filler, and apply this with a plastic spatula as illustrated until the level is above the surrounding metal.

If the dent is localized, it is usually a mistake to attempt to tap it out. The metal has probably been stretched, and too enthusiastic attempts at amateur panel-beating will turn the dent into a bulge—which must then be tapped back again so that the hollow can be built-up with body filler!

In the case of a large, shallow dent, however, the metal may simply have bulged inwards and can be persuaded to spring out again by applying pressure to the inside of the panel. When the inner side cannot be reached — for example in a double-skinned section of the body — the simplest plan is to drill a hole at the centre of the dent, insert a self-tapping screw and pull the dent out by gripping the head of the screw with a pair of pliers, a self-locking wrench, or a claw hammer. The hole can then be filled with stopper, sanded down and touched-in. Another ploy that has proved successful is to ease a deflated football bladder between the two skins of the bodywork, pump it up and pop the dent out.

3 Rubbing down the filler

Here the filler is being rubbed down with progressively finer paper, after the paste has hardened, until a good finish is obtained, to prepare the surface for spraying as described in Sections 8 and 9.

4 Dealing with badly-rusted panels

The corroded metal must be ruthlessly cut away until sound, bright metal is reached. When rust has attacked the back of a panel this may mean that an innocuous-looking pimpled area is converted into a fairly large hole with ragged edges, as shown in the photograph. These must be tapped back with a hammer to about ¼ in. below the level of the surrounding paintwork.

5 Glass-fibre repairs

A typical glass-fibre kit is shown in this photograph. It contains a supply of glass-fibre mat, which is used to cover the damaged area, tissue and ribbon to repair smaller areas, resin, hardener and filler powder, and often a stippling brush, a stirring rod and a mixing bowl.

If the damaged area is a load-bearing one, the only safe repair is to have a patch welded in by a garage. You can then save money by filling and spraying the repaired area at home. If the part is unstressed, however, the sound edges should be tapped in until they are about ¼ in. below the surface of the surrounding metal and a glass-fibre patch can be applied.

6 Applying the glass-fibre mat

Here we show a piece of glass-fibre mat being applied to the damaged area. It is essential to follow the instructions which are supplied with each kit. The principle is to cut a suitably sized piece of mat, mix some resin and catalyst in the correct proportions, stipple the resin generously over the damaged area, apply the glass mat, thoroughly soak this with resin, and repeat the operation with a second layer of mat.

If the damage is fairly extensive, a sheet of perforated zinc can be used to reinforce the glass-fibre. When repairing a rusty hollow section, a self-foaming plastic can be poured into the cavity until it overflows from the

hole, quickly setting into a sufficiently rigid mass to provide a good support for the glass-fibre mat.

7 Preparing for spraying

When the resin has hardened, build up the external surface with the filler paste as shown in the picture.

Use coarse emery paper, an emery disc in an electric drill, or a Surform file to obtain the correct profile. Then rub down the surface with 180 grade wet-or-dry emery paper, used wet, to blend the repair into the surrounding paintwork, followed by light rubbing with 400 grade, again used wet, and preferably with a trace of soap, until a silky smooth surface can be felt.

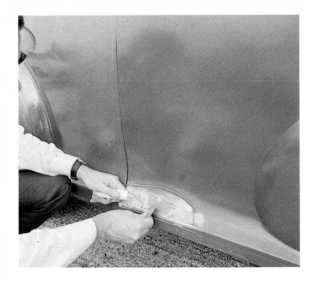

8 Masking-off and spraying

Special masking tape can be obtained from garages and accessory shops. Never use ordinary cellulose tape, which will lift during spraying. Tape around the area to be sprayed, and attach sheets of newspaper to this tape with a second strip of tape, as shown.

Allow sufficient space to blend-in the new paint gradually. If you spray right up to the masking tape, the paint will build up along the edge of the tape and leave a ridge when it is removed.

Aerosol paint spray cans are ideal for small jobs, but first practise spraying on a sheet of metal or hardboard. Spray guns are more expensive and call for experience to obtain really good results.

Wash the prepared surface and allow it to dry before applying at least two coats of primer. Keep the spraying nozzle about 6-9 in. away from the surface, as shown in the photograph. Rub down each coat with 400 grade paper. The first colour coat can then be sprayed on, again followed by a light rub down, before the next coat is applied. Apply further light coats until a good finish is obtained.

Blend the spray into the surrounding paintwork. The colour of the new paint will usually change slightly as it dries and the true colour may not be obtained until a day or so has elapsed.

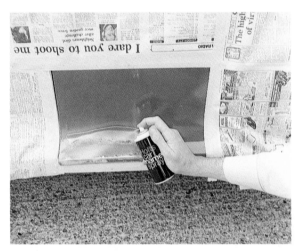

9 Blending and polishing

After the new paint has hardened thoroughly—allow at least a week for this—the surface can be polished and blended in with the old paintwork by using a mild abrasive compound. Liquid metal polish, or one of the 'cleaners' sold by the car polish firms for removing the stale outer film from the paintwork (such as Colour Cut) will produce a good finish.

7 The Ministry Test
Will your car pass or fail?

When you submit your car for the MOT test, the chances are about one in three that it will fail at the first attempt.

This is, of course, an average failure rate for all the cars tested in Great Britain. A more encouraging aspect is that an experienced tester will tell you that in many cases these failures need never have occurred. The faults could have been detected by a practical owner and should have been put right before the car was taken to the testing station.

The value of the test is that it is essentially a safety check. Think of it, if you like, as an expert second opinion on the efficiency of your servicing during the past twelve months, covering such vital points as the brakes, steering, tyres, seat belts and the lighting system. Approach it in this spirit and you will give your car the best chance of passing with flying colours.

In the space available here it is not possible to give a detailed, point-by-point summary of the requirements laid down in the comprehensive Ministry tester's manual (which is revised from time to time to include additional items) but it *is* possible to provide an overall picture of the sort of checks that you can carry out at home.

A surprisingly large number of cars do not get even as far as a detailed inspection. The tester may fail your car if he finds any of the following faults —

Failure of the horn, windscreen wipers and washers to work; stop-lamps which have broken or dirty lenses or faulty bulbs (when two lamps are fitted they must light up simultaneously); direction indicators which do not flash at the correct rate of 60–120 flashes per minute, or have a faulty indicator light; a rusty or perforated exhaust pipe or silencer; shock absorbers which are so worn as to affect the controllability of the car; and bodywork faults such as loose or broken seat mountings, a faulty door lock or bonnet catch, or damaged or torn sections which might injure other road users.

Before going further, you might ask yourself, 'If this were a car belonging to a stranger, would I be completely happy to drive it?'

It you have carried out the checks described in Chapter 3, however, have, preferably, filled in a condition report sheet on the lines suggested in Chapter 5, and have conscientiously carried out the regular servicing outlined in Chapter 4, you should be able to face the test with confidence and we can now turn to some of the detailed checks which can be carried out at home. These form, in effect, a 'dummy run' for the actual test itself.

Checking the braking system

Begin by checking the 'feel' of the brake pedal, with the engine running if a servo is fitted. A 'spongy' pedal, or the need to pump it to take up excessive travel, will call for immediate investigation. Refer to Chart No. 9 to diagnose the most likely causes and turn to Chapter 15 for advice on how to put them right.

Next get under the car, and with an inspection lamp go over the flexible hoses, every inch of the rigid pipelines and the unions. Look for cracks in the hoses, corrosion of the pipelines and seepage of fluid from the unions. Make sure that there is no risk of the hoses being rubbed by the front wheels on full lock and that none of the rigid pipes is in danger of being chafed where it passes close to the underframe or through an opening. Pay particular attention to the handbrake operating cables and rods, looking for frayed cables, worn pivots and clevis pins, and any signs of binding in the mechanism.

Seepage of brake fluid or grease from the wheel bearings on to the brake drums, backplates, discs and calipers will immediately be obvious and would be an equally immediate cause for failing the car.

Check the handbrake for excessive travel and make sure that the ratchet holds securely.

The tester will pay particular attention to all these points before carrying out a brake test. You will not be able to measure the efficiency of the brakes — the minimum is 50% for the foot brake and 25% for the handbrake — but by testing the brakes at about 30 mph on a smooth-surfaced, traffic-free road you should be able to detect any lack of efficiency or a tendency to pull to one side or the other, or to lock one wheel prematurely.

A final point: before handing the car over to the tester, make sure that the brake fluid reservoir has been topped-up to the correct level.

Steering checks

It is reasonable to suppose that you would not allow

your car to go for test if there was an obvious fault such as excessive lost motion at the steering wheel, tight steering, poor self-centring, a tendency to pull to one side or wheel-wobble. Apart from steering faults, one cannot rule out poor roadholding due to weak dampers or a generally tired suspension system.

Check through the symptoms listed in Chart No. 8 and then turn to Chapters 14 and 15 for the corrective action.

The Ministry inspection is not confined to the road test. The tester will raise the car on a lift, or place it over a pit and with the front wheels supported clear of the ground, will push, pull and tug at all the steering connections in order to detect worn joints or loose mountings.

You can forestall him by jacking up each wheel in turn, grasping it at the top and bottom and rocking it to show up excess play in the wheel bearings and in the hub-carrier swivel joints. There should be just perceptible end-play in the wheel bearings. Any excessive movement calls for investigation. Next spin the wheel and listen for grinding or rubbing noises which would indicate that the bearings are badly worn or are breaking up.

With both wheels lowered to the ground, get under the car and ask a friend to tug the steering wheel towards each lock in turn and release it, while you closely watch the steering joints for any signs of wear.

Nowadays, the joints are of the self-adjusting type, except where rubber bushes are used. It used to be said that if any slackness could be felt when the upper part of the joint was levered away from the lower part, replacement was indicated. Many modern joints, however, have a small amount of 'lift' when new, in order to increase their service life. With this type of joint, if the lower half can be raised by more than about 0.01 in. by exerting pressure with a lever pivoted against the inside of the wheel rim, renewal is probably necessary.

You may find that an eccentric type joint is fitted, however, which must be checked for wear by levering it *sideways* in relation to the ball-pin.

Obviously, accurate assessment of the amount of wear which is present calls for experience and that is why we recommend that the best check is to watch the joints while the steering wheel is tugged towards each lock and released. Sloppy joints will immediately show up under this treatment.

If the protective rubber boot on a joint is found to be damaged or displaced, the joint should be renewed as a safety precaution. The tester will probably condemn it, anyway.

The tyres

It should be obvious that tyres which are worn below the legal minimum of 1 mm of tread depth across at least three-quarters of the width of the tread, and around the whole of the circumference of the tyre, are potentially lethal and should not be found on a well-maintained car.

Not so obvious, however, are cuts or bulges on the inner walls of the tyres, or a damaged wheel rim which could cut the tyre or cause sudden loss of pressure. The tester will also look for uneven tread wear, which suggests steering or braking defects, and will immediately fail the car if he discovers an illegal mixture of cross-ply and radial-ply covers. If the tyres are of different types, the radials must always be fitted to the rear wheels. Obviously, it is best to avoid any mixture and stick to cross-plies or radials throughout.

Remember to check the spare wheel. The tester must assume that if you carry a spare you intend to use it if a puncture occurs, and it is therefore logical to fail the car if the spare wheel is fitted with a badly-worn or otherwise defective tyre, or one of the wrong type.

Bodywork condition

The tester will pay particular attention to the underside of the vehicle. Vital components in this respect are the underframes, stressed body sills, suspension mountings and the floor pans, especially where the seat mountings and seat belt attachments are bolted through.

Never be tempted to try to camouflage badly-rusted, stressed areas by glass-fibre repairs. An experienced tester will spot this immediately and will refuse to pass the car until a proper repair has been made by welding-in new sections.

The lighting system

The requirements laid down in the tester's manual can be summed-up in a few words: all the lights on the car which are required by the Construction and Use Regulations must be working properly and the headlamps must be correctly aligned so that they do not dazzle other drivers when dipped.

So far as the standard lighting system is concerned, therefore, all that you have to do is to check for a 'blown' bulb, a wiring fault, a poor earth contact or a faulty switch which prevents a light functioning, a cracked or missing lamp glass or a badly-rusted reflector.

It is not really practical to attempt to adjust the headlamp beams by aiming them at marks on a wall. There are too many sources of error and a proper check can be carried out so much more accurately by a garage, using an optical beam setter. If you have any doubts, have this check made before submitting the car for the test.

The seat belts

Finally, don't forget to check the seat belts and their mountings. The tester is justified in failing a car if he finds a loose or insecure mounting or a badly-frayed belt.

Part three

8 Strip, repair or replace?
Practical notes on overhauls

'Whip it off and fit a new one!' says the garage mechanic or a knowledgeable friend dogmatically when a fault develops in a component which calls for more than a minor repair — and with high labour charges in mind you may feel inclined to agree with him.

But is he giving you good advice? Does it always make economic sense, for example, to fit a service-exchange dynamo or starter motor? The answer is probably 'No,' if all that is required is a set of new brushes and cleaning up the commutator — but the works-reconditioned component has been fully overhauled and *does* carry a guarantee!

In the case of an alternator, on the other hand, it is almost certainly best to fit an exchange unit. It is possible to change the alternator brushes, but testing the diodes and the charging regulator should be left to a qualified auto-electrician.

Where safety is involved we think it better to renew all doubtful items. The hydraulic components in the braking system should be replaced as complete assemblies, for example, instead of trying to salvage them by fitting new rubber parts from an overhaul kit. New rubbers in scored or corroded bores can have very short lives! The same principle applies to steering gear parts.

Again, where the clutch is concerned, renew everything that can wear — in this case as a matter of sound economics. It is much too time-consuming to remove and strip the clutch later should a worn part fail.

Similarly, when you strip a worn gearbox you will probably end up by replacing most of the parts, so there may not be much difference between the cost of these and the price of a reconditioned exchange unit.

In subsequent chapters, and in the notes on engine overhaul which follow, we deal with this subject more fully, indicating those jobs which are likely to be beyond the skill or the resources of the beginner, and suggesting 'repair by replacement' where this is likely to be more economical or more satisfactory.

A final point to bear in mind is that if special service tools will be needed to carry out an overhaul properly, the expense of these — assuming that they cannot be borrowed or hired — will seldom be justified for a one-off job.

Practical aspects of engine overhauls

It is possible to tackle virtually any degree of engine wear in the home garage by dividing the work into three stages and taking advantage of the replacement or reconditioned part or assemblies which are available from specialist firms. The practical aspects of the work are fully covered in Chapter 9, so we can confine ourselves here to a brief discussion of the pros and cons of the various stages of overhaul, which can be summarized as follows —

Stage 1. Fitting new piston rings, including special oil-control rings, to the existing pistons.

Stage 2. Partial overhaul, including new special pistons with rings and gudgeon pins, fitting new connecting-rod bearings, exhaust valves, valve springs and timing chain.

Stage 3. Full overhaul, including fitting a rebored or linered cylinder block, a reground crankshaft, new bearing shells, a reconditioned flywheel with new starter ring, plus other work as Stage 2. Alternatively, fitting a 'half-engine' or 'short-motor' or a 'pin-up' (these terms will be described later) or a fully-reconditioned power unit.

Even if you are a novice, you should be able to tackle Stages 1 and 2 with every prospect of success. If you have had some experience of working on engines, there is no reason why you should not carry out the more ambitious Stage 3 overhaul, provided that you are able to borrow or hire lifting tackle to remove and refit the engine (don't rely on the roof beam of a prefabricated garage to carry the weight of the engine) and can call on the assistance of a friend when an extra pair of hands is needed.

Bearing in mind these points, a brief run through the pros and cons of the different reconditioning methods may help you to come to the right decision.

Fitting new piston rings (Stage 1)

A set of special piston rings can deal successfully with bore wear up to a maximum of about 0.004 in. for each inch of cylinder diameter, but their effectiveness depends on correct fitting.

It is usually necessary to send the pistons to the firm that supplies the rings so that the worn grooves can be machined to match the new rings. If the grooves are badly worn — particularly the top compression ring grooves — it may be necessary to fit groove inserts.

Never be tempted to fit a set of oil-control rings to worn pistons without enlisting the help of a specialist supplier. At best, the result may be disappointing; at worst, ring breakage may occur, scoring the cylinder walls and rendering a rebore essential.

Oil consumption should remain within reasonable limits for about 10 000 miles after a Stage 1 overhaul. If it is proposed to sell or exchange the car within this mileage, therefore, the fitting of special rings alone may well be an economic proposition.

Stage 2 overhaul

If you intend to keep the car for a longer period, however, and it has not covered more than about 40 000-60 000 miles, serious consideration should be given to a Stage 2 overhaul.

Most of the work entailed will be the same as that required when fitting new rings alone but the replacement of the pistons and the connecting-rod bearings, combined with a top-overhaul and the fitting of new exhaust valves, and a set of valve springs, will give the engine a new lease of life.

'Intermediate engine overhaul' kits are available from specialist firms such as AE Edmunds Walker and can be ordered through your garage. They contain everything that is needed for a Stage 2 overhaul—pistons and rings, bearing shells, exhaust valves, valve springs, gaskets, jointing compound and even an oil filter and a piston-ring clamp.

If the cylinder bore wear exceeds about 0.004 in. per inch of cylinder diameter, however — say, ten thousandths in a 2½-inch cylinder, which is a considerable amount of wear by modern standards — fitting special pistons and rings is unlikely to be effective. This calls for a Stage 3 overhaul.

Stage 3 overhaul

The simplest solution is to lift the engine out and install a reconditioned unit; or you can go to the other extreme and strip it right down, fit new or reconditioned parts as necessary and rebuild it.

If you decide to fit a 'recon' engine, you again have the choice of ordering a factory-rebuilt unit from your local dealer, or shopping around for a rebuilt engine at a lower price among the smaller engineering firms which specialize in this work. The advertisements in the practical motoring papers will provide a list of prospects.

The fact that the prices charged by these firms are generally lower than the cost of an engine which has been rebuilt by the car manufacturer does not necessarily mean that the units are of lower quality. A specialist rebuilder does not have to carry the heavy overheads of a car manufacturer, nor does he have to allow a sizeable commission to a local dealer who supplies the engine.

Reputable engine rebuilding firms usually offer a worthwhile guarantee, however. In such cases their units should be just as satisfactory as factory-rebuilt units.

Although these are known in the trade as 'full' engines, they are not in fact complete. You will have to remove the carburettor, manifolds, ignition distributor, starter, fuel pump and possibly the water pump from your engine and fit them to the new unit — after suitably reconditioning them, of course.

It will probably be necessary also to remove and keep the securing studs, bolts and nuts for these items, which will not be supplied with the new unit. In some cases you may have to fit your own flywheel and valve cover, so check carefully just what is offered.

A cheaper proposition is the 'half engine' or 'short motor.' This consists of a rebored cylinder block, fitted with a reground crankshaft in new main bearings, complete with reconditioned connecting rods, new pistons and rings, a reground camshaft, new or refaced cam followers and new timing sprockets. To this you add your own reconditioned cylinder head, the auxiliaries already mentioned and the other bits and pieces that go to make up the complete engine.

A short engine obviously entails a good deal more work on your part, but with a corresponding saving in expense. Few, if any, special tools are required and all the skilled work has been done for you.

Finally, the cheapest proposition is that known in the trade as a 'pin-up'—which sounds interesting, but in fact means simply that the parts supplied are limited to a reconditioned cylinder block, pistons, crankshaft and connecting rods, ready-assembled for you to build into a complete engine, using your own new and reconditioned parts for the remaining items.

The time factor

If this is to be your first attempt at carrying out, say, a partial engine overhaul, make sure that you allow plenty of time, plus a safety margin for unexpected delays. If you begin work on a Friday evening, it should be possible to complete the preliminary dismantling of the cylinder head that night, so that any replacements that are found to be necessary and are not included in the intermediate engine overhaul kit referred to earlier can be obtained on Saturday morning, when most garages and spares counters are open.

By making an early start on Saturday it should be possible to lift the engine out, withdraw the connecting rods and pistons, remove the old pistons and fit the replacements, reassemble the pistons and connecting rods (fitted with new bearing shells) in the cylinders and finally turn your attention to decarbonizing the cylinder head and grinding-in the valves.

The whole of Sunday will probably be occupied in finishing off the bottom half of the engine, fitting a new filter, refitting the cylinder head, manifolds and carburettor, reinstalling the engine and making adjustments, followed by a short test run.

9 The engine

Until October 1962, the Minor 1000 was fitted with the British Leyland 948 cc 'A' series engine which has earned an enviable reputation for reliability in a wide range of Leyland models.

A 1098 cc version of the engine was used subsequently — basically the same as the earlier model, but with detail differences to which we refer in the appropriate sections of this chapter, where they affect maintenance and overhaul.

Strictly speaking, perhaps, the later car should have been renamed the Minor 1100, but the old description was retained.

A conventional overhead-valve layout is used on both engines, the valves being operated by rockers and push-rods from a camshaft in the cylinder block, driven by a roller chain and sprockets from the nose of the crankshaft. The cylinder block and crankcase components are also of conventional design.

The pistons are of the four-ring pattern — three compression rings and one oil-control ring. The connecting-rod big-ends and the main bearings are fitted with replaceable steel-backed thin-shell bearings, which can be renewed without the need for special fitting.

Routine engine maintenance

The jobs described in this section are those listed in the maintenance schedule. Engine maintenance, of course, also includes a certain amount of work on the cooling system, the carburettor and petrol pump and the ignition system. These jobs are dealt with in Chapters 10, 11 and 12.

Engine lubrication

The oil level should be checked with the car standing on level ground. A few minutes should be allowed for oil to drain back to the sump to prevent a misleadingly low reading being shown. Remove the dipstick, wipe it, return it and push it fully home before withdrawing it to check the level.

It is more economical to keep the sump well topped-up than to allow the level to fall to near the danger point, at the end of the dipstick, before restoring the level. Remember, too, that the oil consumption will be increased in hot weather and may be quite substantially increased when long, fast runs are undertaken, as compared with the figure that one becomes

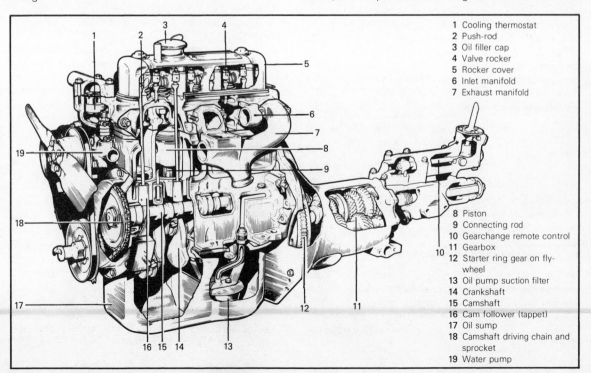

1 Cooling thermostat
2 Push-rod
3 Oil filler cap
4 Valve rocker
5 Rocker cover
6 Inlet manifold
7 Exhaust manifold

8 Piston
9 Connecting rod
10 Gearchange remote control
11 Gearbox
12 Starter ring gear on flywheel
13 Oil pump suction filter
14 Crankshaft
15 Camshaft
16 Cam follower (tappet)
17 Oil sump
18 Camshaft driving chain and sprocket
19 Water pump

Fig. 9.1. A typical Minor 1000 engine and gearbox assembly

accustomed to when shorter runs at modest speeds are the order of the day. Tests have shown that the oil does not attain its maximum temperature until the car has been running for approximately one hour.

Oil warning lights

The oil-pressure warning light in the speedometer dial should glow whenever the ignition is first switched on. If it does not do so, the trouble should be investigated as soon as possible. This light is controlled by an oil-pressure-operated switch, which is adjusted so that if the oil pressure falls below a safe figure the light will glow as a warning to the driver.

Obviously this warning should never be ignored; the car should not be driven until the oil level in the sump has been checked and the lubrication system tested by connecting a pressure gauge to the warning light switch union — a job which can be done by practically any garage.

The pressure shown under normal running conditions should not fall below about 60 lb/sq in. About 15 lb/sq in. should be recorded when the engine is idling.

If the warning light flickers on and off when the car is driven fast around corners the indication is that the oil level in the sump is dangerously low and that the oil is surging away from the intake to the oil pump. This obviously is a danger signal which cannot be ignored. The car should be driven as quietly as possible until the normal sump oil level can be restored.

On later models a second oil warning lamp is provided (on the left of the speedometer) which lights up only when the oil filter element is becoming clogged and is due for replacement. The increased resistance caused by a dirty filter operates a switch on the filter housing. This switch proved troublesome and if it has packed-up it should be left out of action. Simply change the filter element at 6000-mile intervals.

9.1 Engine oil change

The sump should be drained when the car has just come in from a run, when the oil is hot and fluid.

1 Remove the drain plug.

2 Allow sufficient time for the oil to drain completely before replacing the plug.

3 While the oil is draining clean the drain plug.

4 Refill the sump with fresh oil, up to the 'Max' mark on the dipstick.

9.2 Changing the oil filter element

The oil filter element should be changed after 6000 miles or six months, whichever is the sooner. If the warning light fitted to later models glows before this mileage or time has elapsed, however, the filter should be changed as soon as possible; certainly within the next 300 miles.

Fig. 9.2 The underside of the engine and gearbox. 1, gearbox drain plug. 2, engine sump drain plug. 3, oil filter retaining bolt. 4, oil

Normally, the filter casing is removed by working from beneath.

1 Disconnect the battery.

2 Clean the exterior of the casing and the upper casting as thoroughly as possible before removing the central retaining bolt.

3 Hold a tin beneath the filter to catch the oil which will drain out as the bolt is withdrawn. The casing can then be manoeuvred sideways and clear of the engine sump.

4 The new element will be supplied complete with new sealing washers. The sealing washer in the casting against which the upper edge of the filter bowl seats should, strictly speaking, be renewed, but it is a tricky job to fit the new washer evenly into its groove. If the old washer appears to be in good condition, therefore, it is best to leave well alone. Only if an oil leak becomes apparent when the filter is reassembled and this cannot be corrected by slackening the bolt and repositioning the filter, should the washer be renewed.

5 Thoroughly clean the filter bowl before the new element is inserted. Position the small felt washer between the element pressure plate and the metal washer above the pressure spring. To ensure correct oil filtration it is particularly important that this washer should be in good condition and a snug fit on the central securing bolt.

6 As soon as the engine is running, examine the filter for leakage. A very pronounced oil leak will occur if the bowl is slightly displaced and does not seat squarely on the sealing ring.

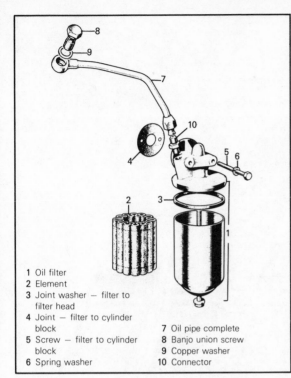

1 Oil filter
2 Element
3 Joint washer — filter to filter head
4 Joint — filter to cylinder block
5 Screw — filter to cylinder block
6 Spring washer
7 Oil pipe complete
8 Banjo union screw
9 Copper washer
10 Connector

Fig. 9.3 The oil filter components

9.3 Checking the valve tappet clearances

In order to maintain any engine in good tune, it is essential to check the valve tappet clearances at regular intervals.

The correct clearances between the ends of the rockers and the tops of the valve stems are given in Chapter 17. They can be measured with the engine hot or cold during the course of normal servicing, but should be re-checked when the engine is hot if any part of the valve gear has been dismantled and reassembled. *Never check the clearances when the engine is warm,* as misleading results will be obtained.

To check and adjust the clearances —

1 Remove the rocker cover, but before doing so it is best to buy a new gasket. There is a risk of damaging the old one, and in any case, a gasket which has been compressed in service may not make a satisfactory seal when the rocker cover is replaced. Even a slight oil leak can result in a very messy engine.

2 To make sure that each tappet is on the base of its cam while the clearance of the corresponding valve is being adjusted, use the 'rule of 9,' as follows: check No. 1 valve with No. 8 fully open; No. 3 with No. 6 fully open; No. 5 with No. 4 fully open; and so on, using pairs of valves which add up to 9.

3 Slide a feeler gauge between the tip of the valve stem and the end of the rocker. If the clearance is correct, the blade should be a light drag fit — not too tight, and not too loose.

4 If adjustment is needed, slacken the lock-nut at the push-rod end of the rocker (preferably with a ring spanner, as the edges of the flats on the nut can be easily burred-over by an open-jawed spanner). Turn the adjusting screw with a screwdriver to give a correct clearance and hold the screw in position while tightening the lock-nut.

5 Check the clearance again. The action of tightening the nut will probably have altered it.

6 Replace the rocker cover. Tighten the retaining screws evenly and progressively and then run the engine for a few minutes to make sure that there is no oil leakage past the gasket.

Engine overhauls

Most of the repairs and replacements which are likely to be undertaken by a d.i.y. owner can be tackled without removing the engine from the car, including such jobs as top-overhauls, renewing the crankshaft front oil seal and fitting new pistons and connecting-rod bearings during the course of a partial overhaul of the type described in Chapter 8.

For a complete strip, of course, it is necessary to remove the engine as described in Section 9.14, but owing to the simple construction of the power unit, dismantling and reassembly should be within the scope of any practical owner.

It must be assumed that an owner who is prepared to tackle major overhauls will have had some experience of engine dismantling, fitting and assembly or will be able to rely on the guidance of an experienced mechanic. The various stages of overhaul are discussed in Chapter 8.

Fig. 9.4 Adjusting the valve clearances. The feeler gauge, 1, is inserted between the tip of the valve stem and the rocker. One of the adjusting screws, locked by a lock nut, is shown at 2

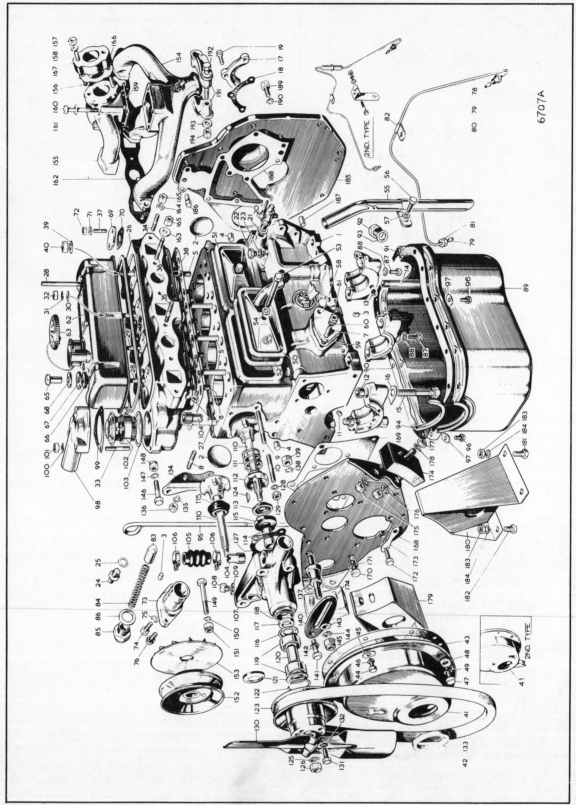

Fig. 9.5 The Minor 1000 cylinder head, cylinder block, crankcase and manifold assemblies

No.	Description
1	Block – cylinder
2	Plug – core hole
3	Plug – oil relief valve passage
4	Plug – oil gallery
5	Stud – long – cylinder head
6	Stud – short – cylinder head
7	Stud – blanking plate
8	Stud – rear dynamo bracket
9	Stud – long – water pump body
10	Stud – short – water pump body
11	Restrictor – camshaft oil feed
12	Dowel – main bearing cap
13	Plug – rear main bearing cap
14	Pipe – rear main bearing cap drain
15	Bolt – main bearing cap
16	Lock washer – bolt
17	Cover – rear
18	Joint – cover
19	Screw – cover
20	Tap – water drain
21	Washer – tap
22	Plug – oil priming
23	Washer – copper – plug
24	Union – oil gauge pipe
25	Washer – copper – union
26	Cylinder head
27	Plug – oil hole
28	Stud – long – rocker bracket
29	Stud – short – rocker bracket
30	Washer – rocker bracket stud
31	Spring washer – rocker bracket stud
32	Nut – rocker bracket stud
33	Stud – water outlet elbow
34	Stud – short – exhaust manifold
35	Stud – medium – exhaust manifold
36	Stud – long – exhaust manifold
37	Stud – heater tap hole plate
38	Joint – cylinder head
39	Washer – cylinder head stud
40	Nut – cylinder head stud
41	Cover – cylinder block front
42	Felt – cover
43	Joint – cover
44	Screw – to front bearer plate
45	Washer – plain – screw
46	Spring washer – screw
47	Screw – to bearer plate and block
48	Washer – plain – screw
49	Spring washer – screw
50	Cover with elbow – front – block side
51	Cover – rear – block side
52	Joint – covers
53	Screw – to block
54	Washer – fibre – screw
55	Pipe – with clip – fume vent
56	Screw – clip
57	Spring washer – screw
58	Plate – blanking
59	Joint – to block
60	Spring washer – stud
61	Nut – stud
62	Cover – rocker gear
63	Cap with cable
64	Joint – cover
65	Cap nut
66	Bush – rubber – cap nut
67	Cup washer – nut
68	Washer – bracket – height adjusting
69	Cover-plate – heater control tap
70	Joint – cover plate
71	Spring washer – cover-plate stud
72	Nut – stud
73	Housing – distributor
74	Screw – to block
75	Washer – shakeproof – screw
76	Screw – distributor to housing
77	Pipe – ignition control
78	Olive – pipe
79	Nut – pipe – carburetter end
80	Nut – pipe – distributor end
81	Clip – pipe
82	Valve – oil relief
83	Spring-valve
84	Cap – valve
85	Washer – fibre – cap
86	Screw – to bearing cap
87	Washer – shakeproof – screw
88	Sump
89	Joint – R.H. – sump
90	Joint – L.H. – sump
91	Plug – drain
92	Washer – plug
93	Seal – main bearing cap
94	Indicator – oil level
95	Screw – to block
96	Washer – screw
97	Washer – screw
98	Elbow – water outlet
99	Joint – elbow
100	Spring washer – stud
101	Nut – stud
102	Thermostat
103	Joint – thermostat
104	Adaptor – by-pass
105	Connection – adaptor
106	Clip – connection
107	Body – water pump
108	Plug – body
109	Washer – fibre – plug
110	Spindle with vane
111	Spring
112	Cup – spring locating
113	Seal – rubber
114	Distance piece
115	Seal
116	Retainer – outer – for felt
117	Felt
118	Retainer – inner – for felt
119	Bearing
120	Distance piece – bearing
121	Retainer – bearing grease
122	Circlip – retainer
123	Pulley
124	Key – pulley
125	Washer – spindle
126	Nut – spindle
127	Joint – to block
128	Spring washer – pump stud
129	Nut – pump stud
130	Blade – fan
131	Screw – to pulley
132	Spring washer – screw
133	Belt – fan
134	Bracket – dynamo – rear
135	Spring washer – bracket stud
136	Nut – bracket stud
137	Pillar – adjusting link
138	Spring washer – pillar
139	Nut – pillar
140	Link – dynamo adjusting
141	Screw – link to dynamo
142	Spring washer – screw
143	Washer – link to pillar
144	Spring washer – link to pillar
145	Nut – link to pillar
146	Bolt – dynamo to bracket
147	Spring washer – bolt
148	Nut – bolt
149	Bolt – dynamo to water pump body
150	Spring washer – bolt
151	Nut – bolt
152	Pulley – dynamo
153	Fan – dynamo
154	Manifold – exhaust
155	Manifold – inlet
156	Stud – carburetter
157	Nut – stud
158	Washer – stud
159	Joint – manifolds
160	Bolt – inlet to exhaust
161	Washer – bolt
162	Joint – to block
163	Washer – large – clamping
164	Washer – small
165	Nut – stud
166	Distance piece – to manifold
167	Joint – carburetter
168	Plate – front bearer
169	Joint – to block
170	Screw – to block
171	Spring washer – screw
172	Screw – to main bearing cap
173	Plate – locking – cap screw
174	Block – rubber – front mounting
175	Nut – to plate
176	Spring washer – nut
177	Nut – to front mounting bracket
178	Spring washer – nut
179	Bracket – front mounting – R.H.
180	Bracket – front mounting – L.H.
181	Bolt – to frame
182	Screw – to frame
183	Nut – for bolt or screw
184	Spring washer – nut
185	Plate – rear bearer-gearbox
186	Dowel – top – to block
187	Dowel – bottom – to block
188	Joint – to block
189	Screw – to block
190	Spring washer – screw
191	Clamp – exhaust to manifold
192	Bolt – clamp
193	Washer – bolt
194	Nut – bolt

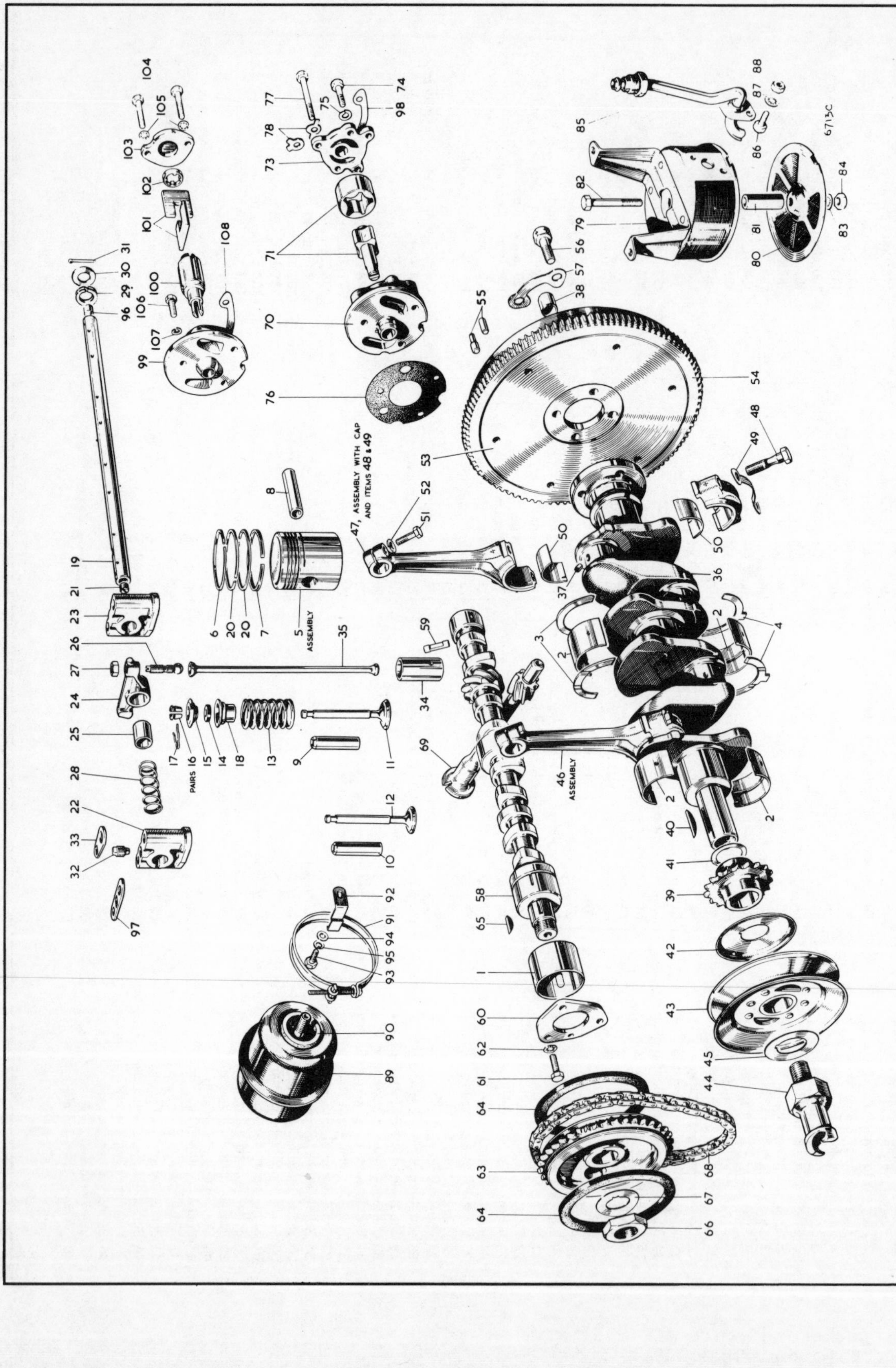

Fig. 9.6 The moving parts of the Minor 1000 engine

1 Liner – front camshaft bearing
2 Bearing – crankshaft main
3 Thrust washer – upper – crankshaft
4 Thrust washer – lower – crankshaft
5 Piston assembly
6 Ring – compression – piston – first and third
7 Ring – scraper – piston – bottom
8 Pin – gudgeon
9 Guide – inlet valve
10 Guide – exhaust valve
11 Valve-Inlet
12 Valve – exhaust
13 Spring – valve
14 Oil seal – valve
15 Cup – valve spring
15 Cup – valve spring
16 Retainer – valve cap
17 Circlip – valve retainer
18 Shroud – guide and oil seal retainer
19 Shaft – valve rocker
20 Ring – compression – piston – second
21 Plug – screwed – rocker shaft
22 Bracket – tapped hole – shaft
23 Bracket – shaft
24 Rocker – valve
25 Bush – rocker
26 Screw – tappet adjusting

27 Locknut – adjusting screw
28 Spring – rocker
29 Washer – D/C – rocker
30 Washer – plain – rocker
31 Split pin – rocker
32 Screw – rocker locating
33 Plate – locating screw
34 Tappet – valve
35 Push-rod – tappet
36 Crankshaft
37 Restrictor – crankshaft – oil
38 Bush – drive gear
39 Gear – crankshaft
40 Key – gear and pulley
41 Washer – gear packing
42 Thrower – crankshaft oil
43 Pulley – crankshaft
44 Nut – starting-handle dog
45 Lock washer-nut
46 Rod and cap – connecting – 1 and 3
47 Rod and cap – connecting – 2 and 4
48 Bolt – cap
49 Lock washer – cap bolt
50 Bearing – connecting rod
51 Screw gudgeon pin clamp
52 Spring washer – clamp screw
53 Flywheel

54 Ring – flywheel starter
55 Dowel – flywheel to clutch
56 Screw – flywheel to crankshaft
57 Lock washer – screw
58 Camshaft
59 Pin – oil pump drive
60 Plate – camshaft locating
61 Screw – plate to block
62 Washer – shakeproof – screw
63 Gear – camshaft
64 Ring – gear tensioner
65 Key – gear
66 Nut – camshaft
67 Lock washer – nut
68 Chain – timing
69 Spindle – distributor drive
70 Body – oil pump
71 Shaft with inner rotor – pump
73 Cover – pump
74 Screw – pump cover
75 Spring washer – screw
76 Joint – pump to block
77 Bolt – pump to block
78 Lock washer – bolt
79 Body with bracket – oil strainer
80 Cover – strainer body
81 Distance piece – strainer

82 Bolt – cover
83 Washer – shakeproof – bolt
84 Nut – bolt
85 Pipe – oil suction
86 Screw – pipe to strainer
87 Washer – shakeproof screw
88 Nut – screw
89 Filter (external)
90 Ring – filter – sealing
91 Clip – filter – locking
92 Bracket – filter
93 Screw – bracket to block
94 Washer – backet screw
95 Spring washer – screw
96 Plug – plain
97 Plate – rocker bracket stud
98 Washer – lock
99 Body
100 Rotor
101 Vanes
102 Sleeve – rotor
103 Cover
104 Bolt – cover
105 Washer – bolt
106 Bolt – body
107 Washer – bolt
108 Washer – lock – oil pump

The time factor

It is not always easy to estimate the time required for engine overhaul jobs, since so much depends on the facilities available. The following times, however, are suggested for typical jobs: Partial engine overhaul (see Chapter 8), 2-3 days; top-overhaul and decarbonizing, allow at least one full day — preferably a week-end; remove and refit engine, 10 hr; changing timing chain and fitting new timing cover oil seal, 4 hr; changing engine mountings, 2 hr; fitting new exhaust system, 1 hr; changing oil filter, 15 min.

Decarbonizing and top-overhaul

Removal of the cylinder head, cleaning off deposits of carbon and re-seating the valves is usually termed 'decarbonizing,' although a more correct term, in view of the work involved, is a 'top-overhaul.'

If the job is confined solely to removing and refitting the head — to replace a faulty gasket, for example — only Sections 9.4 and 9.11 apply. A full top-overhaul involves the work covered by Sections 9.4 to 9.11.

The list of materials and tools required which follows covers a complete top-overhaul, but can, of course, be modified to suit the actual stages carried out.

Materials: Gasket set. Water hoses. Set of valve springs. Spare exhaust valves (have at least two in reserve as a safety margin). Valve stem oil seals. Valve-grinding paste. Emery paper. Rags. Paraffin. Tins, jars, boxes for parts. Old piston ring.
Tools: Set spanners. Socket spanners. Screwdriver. Pliers. Blunt scraper for carbon. Wire brush. Valve-spring compressor. Valve-grinding tool. A torque wrench. Electric drill with wire brushes — not essential.

Practical pointers

Here are some practical tips which will help to ensure the success of the job.

If the water hoses are difficult to remove, they can be cut through with a knife. It is best to fit new hoses on reassembly.

The cylinder-head nuts *must* be slackened progressively, working diagonally from the centre of the head outwards. *This is most important to avoid distorting the head.*

Discard the valve springs and fit a new set.

As each valve is withdrawn from its guide, place it in the correct order on the bench. *The valves must not be interchanged.* Punch holes in a strip of cardboard to take the stems and number these to correspond with the positions of the valves in the head.

If the cylinder head does not come away easily, don't attempt to prise it up by inserting a screwdriver or similar tool between the head and the block, as this may damage the machined surfaces. A sharp tap with a wooden mallet, or with a hammer on a block of wood held against the side of the head, should free the joint.

Do not use an abrasive, such as metal polish, on the pistons, owing to the risk of particles being trapped in the piston-ring grooves or between the rings and the cylinder walls.

Most authorities recommend that a narrow ring of carbon should be left around the edge of each piston crown and around the top edge of each cylinder bore, the theory being that these form useful oil seals if the piston rings and bores are no longer in perfect condition. There are conflicting views on this but it does no harm to play safe. This is where an old piston ring comes into the picture: placed on top of the piston, it protects the carbon seals from the scraper and the wire brush.

9.4 Removing the cylinder head

1 Drain the radiator and cylinder block, saving the coolant if it contains anti-freeze and is to be re-used. The system must be drained completely, for partial draining can damage the water-pump seal face on the impellor. This sometimes causes very early failure of the pump seal. Disconnect the top radiator hose and the heater hose. Slacken the clip on the by-pass hose beneath the thermostat housing.

2 Disconnect the battery, remove the air cleaner, disconnect the ignition distributor vacuum-advance pipe and the crankcase breather pipe.

3 Remove the rocker cover.

4 Disconnect the lead from the water-temperature gauge transmitter, pull off the sparking-plug connectors and disconnect the heater pipes. Remove the thermostat housing, take out the thermostat and check its condition — see Section 10.5.

5 Unscrew the bolts which retain the rocker-shaft assembly, and also the cylinder head bolts, evenly in the sequence shown in Fig. 9.8. Lift off the rocker shaft as an assembly.

6 Take out the push-rods, first giving each a sharp twist to break the suction of the oil at its base in the tappet. Place the push-rods in order where they will not be disturbed so that they can be refitted in their original positions. It is a good plan to push them through numbered holes in a sheet of cardboard.

7 Disconnect the petrol-feed pipe. Disconnect the carburettor controls and take off the carburettor.

8 The exhaust pipe should be disconnected at the flange on the exhaust manifold. Cover the open end of the pipe and support it to prevent damage.

9 Remove the nuts which secure the cylinder head to the cylinder block and lift off the head, with the manifolds still attached to it.

9.5 Dismantling the cylinder head

If you do not intend to carry out a top-overhaul — for example, if the only reason for removing the cylinder head is to renew a faulty cylinder-head gasket — the combustion chambers can be decarbonized without further dismantling, although it is better to remove the manifolds to allow the inlet and exhaust ports to be cleaned out. In any event, it is best to decarbonize the combustion chambers before removing the valves, to avoid the risk of damaging the valve seatings in the cylinder head.

During a top-overhaul, of course, it will be necessary to remove the valves for inspection and refacing of the valves and seatings, or renewal of any valves which are in too poor condition to justify refacing and re-fitting them.

To dismantle the cylinder head —

1 Take off the inlet and exhaust manifolds.

2 Dismantle the valve gear and remove the valves, as described in Section 9.7; but if the cylinder head is to be decarbonized, defer removing the valves until the combustion chambers have been cleaned and burnished (see below).

9.6 Decarbonizing the cylinder head

1 Decarbonize the combustion-chamber faces before removing the valves, to avoid any risk of damaging the valve seatings. Scrape off every trace of carbon and burnish the underside of the head with a wire brush.

2 Thoroughly clean the cylinder-block and manifold mating faces of the head, taking particular care not to score them.

9.7 Removing and cleaning the valves

The valve-spring caps are retained by split-cone collets and a valve-spring compressor is needed to remove them.

1 Compress each valve spring with the spring-compressor until the spring cap is clear of the split collets. Remove these and release the spring.

2 Take off the valve-spring retainer, sleeve, spring and the oil seal fitted to an inlet valve. Draw the valve out of its guide.

3 Clean the undersides of the valve heads, the stems and also the ports in the heads which could not be reached when the valves were in position. Be careful not to score the faces of the valves and their seats in the combustion chambers. Wire-wool soap-pads quickly remove carbon.

4 Scrape the valve stems clean. Don't use emery cloth on the sections that work in the guides. Clean out the guides themselves by drawing a paraffin-soaked rag through them.

5 Check each valve for fit in its own guide. If there is any noticeable degree of sideways shake, take the head to your dealer for advice. If he confirms that the valves and guides are worn, allow him to ream the guides, to re-cut the seats in the head and to fit new oversize valves.

9.8 Reseating the valves

If the seating faces on the valves are badly pitted, they can be trued-up by using a valve refacing tool (your garage should be able to do this for you).

Badly-pitted valve seatings in the cylinder head can be refaced with a special tool — normally this is also a job for your garage. If the pitting is only slight, however, the valves can be ground-in in the conventional manner, as described below.

The object of grinding-in the valves (or more correctly, lapping-in) is to obtain a gastight seal between each valve and its seating. The importance of making a really good job of valve-lapping cannot be over-emphasized, since not only the cylinder compressions but the service life of the valves depend on a first class seal between the valves and their seatings.

Valve-grinding paste usually comes in a tin which contains two grades, fine and coarse. The coarse paste should be used only in an emergency, to remove pitting when proper reconditioning cannot be carried out, but light pitting may be removed with the fine paste, grinding being continued until a good matt finish has been obtained on the valve and seat.

1 Smear a little grinding paste on the face of the valve and rotate the valve quickly and lightly on its seat with the suction-cap grinding tool, first in one direction and then in the other, by spinning the handle of the tool between the palms of the hands. From time to time, raise the valve from its seat and turn it through

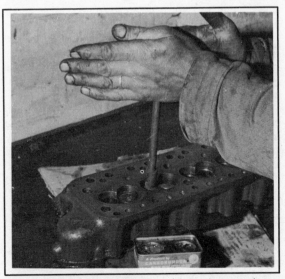

Fig. 9.7 Grinding-in a valve. The handle of the suction-cup tool should be spun between the palms of the hands while light pressure is applied to the head of the valve

a quarter of a turn, before continuing the grinding. This will ensure that an even, concentric surface is obtained. A light coil spring, placed beneath the head of the valve, will make the job easier, as it will lift the valve whenever pressure on it is relaxed.

2 Check the progress of the grinding-in frequently. When correctly ground, both the valve seat in the cylinder head and the face of the valve should have an even, clean, grey matt finish with no signs of bright rings or any evidence of pitting. Bright rings are caused by grinding with insufficient grinding paste, while 'tramlines' are usually the result of continuously grinding the valve on its seat without taking up a different position.

3 Check the effectiveness of the seal by making a series of pencil marks across the face of the valve with a soft lead pencil. Replace the valve and rotate it once through a quarter of a turn on its seat. Each pencil mark should be erased at the line of contact. If any of the lines are unbroken, either the valve or its seat is not truly circular and renewal or refacing of the valve or seat (or both) is required.

4 When grinding-in has been completed, wash the valves and seats with petrol or paraffin, making sure that all traces of grinding paste have been removed. Lubricate the valve stems with a little clean engine oil before refitting them and reassembling the new oil seals, springs and retainers.

9.9 Checking the rockers and rocker shaft

While the rocker and rocker shaft assembly is off, check the rockers for wear in the bushes and for any signs of indentation on the hardened pads which contact the valve stems.

1 Shallow pits on the faces of the rockers can be smoothed off by removing only the metal which stands proud, using an oil-stone or a grinding wheel. Be careful to retain the correct profile and do not grind the recessed section. If the pitting is deep, however — more than about 2-3 thousandths of an inch — the case-hardening on the rockers may have been penetrated and it will be necessary to fit new rockers.

2 Before refacing the rockers, check the fit of each on the rocker shaft, after cleaning the rocker bush and the shaft. If the rocker is a sloppy fit, it will probably be possible also to feel a worn spot on the underside of the shaft. Test each rocker on an unworn section of the shaft and if the fit is reasonable here, only a new shaft may be needed. If the engine has covered a high mileage, however, a new set of rockers will also be required. Any excessive wear on the rockers or the shaft will make it impossible to obtain a quiet engine, even with the tappet clearances correctly adjusted.

3 If the shaft on an early engine is replaced by the later pattern which is located by a setscrew in No. 2 pillar instead of in No. 1, it will be necessary to swap-

over No. 1 and No. 2 pillars — *but it is essential to drill an oil hole in the No. 2 pillar to match that in the No. 1 pillar.* Otherwise the rocker gear will not receive oil from the hole at the front of the cylinder head. Alternatively, fit a new set of the later pillars to match the later shaft.

9.10 Decarbonizing the pistons

1 Rotate the crankshaft until two of the pistons are at the tops of the cylinders.

2 Stuff clean rags into the bores of the remaining cylinders and in the water-ways and other openings in the cylinder block.

3 Remove the carbon from the piston crowns with a suitable blunt scraper, taking care not to score the surfaces. Then burnish the crowns with a wire brush.

9.11 Replacing the cylinder head

Before refitting the cylinder head, make sure that the piston crowns, cylinder walls and the top of the block are scrupulously clean. Pour a small quantity of engine oil around each bore so that it will be distributed over the cylinder walls and down the sides of the pistons when the engine is first rotated.

Do not use gasket cement on the cylinder-head gasket, as this is likely to cause subsequent leakage. A jointing compound such as Wellseal or Hermetite should, however, be used on all other gaskets and sealing washers.

1 Refit the inlet and exhaust manifolds.

2 Lay the gasket on the cylinder block, making sure that it is the correct type, the right way up and that the openings register with the water-transfer holes in the cylinder block.

3 Slide the cylinder head down on to the gasket. The cylinder-head retaining nuts should be tightened progressively, in the sequence shown in Fig. 9.8 to the

Fig. 9.8 The cylinder-head nuts must always be slackened and tightened in the order shown. A similar sequence should be followed when an 11-stud head is fitted

torque quoted in Chapter 17. This is equivalent to a firm pull on a spanner of normal length.

4 Place the push-rods in position, making sure that they locate in their respective tappets.

5 Slacken-off the tappet-adjusting screws fully and fit the rocker-shaft assembly, making sure that the adjusting screws engage properly in the push-rod cups. Tighten the rocker-bracket nuts down evenly, finger-tight, and then tighten the nuts progressively to a torque of 25 lb ft.

6 Adjust the valve clearances as described in Section 9.3.

7 Complete the remainder of the reassembly, which is quite straightforward.

8 Adjust the carburettor controls.

9 After a final check all round, refill the cooling system, start the engine and warm it up. Check the level of the water in the radiator after the engine has been running for a few minutes.

10 When the engine is at its normal running temperature, adjust the carburettor idling speed and mixture strength, as described in Chapter 11.

11 Switch off the engine and check the tightness of the cylinder head and manifold nuts. These should be again checked after about 300 miles of running. Remember to readjust the valve clearances on each occasion, as they will be reduced when the cylinder head is tightened down.

9.12 Renewing the timing chain cover oil seal

Materials: New oil seal. New gasket for timing chain cover.

Tools: Wrench 18G 98A or strong socket with long handle. Spanners. Special tools 18G 134 and 18G 134BD to remove and replace oil seal — desirable but not essential.

1 Remove the radiator and fan belt.

2 Tap back the tab of the crankshaft pulley locking washer.

3 Remove the starter motor and wedge the flywheel by lodging a stout screwdriver in the flywheel ring gear teeth.

4 With a socket and a long bar, undo the pulley retaining bolt. This can be very tight. An alternative method is not to wedge the flywheel but to lodge the tommy-bar of the socket securely and then kick the engine over with the starter motor, thus unwinding the pulley nut.

5 Carefully lever the pulley and damper assembly from the crankshaft.

6 Remove the setscrews and take off the timing chain cover.

7 Lever out the old seal carefully and be sure to keep the new seal absolutely square as you tap it into place with a block of wood. Special service tools are available but not essential if care is taken.

8 Make sure that the oil thrower is fitted with the

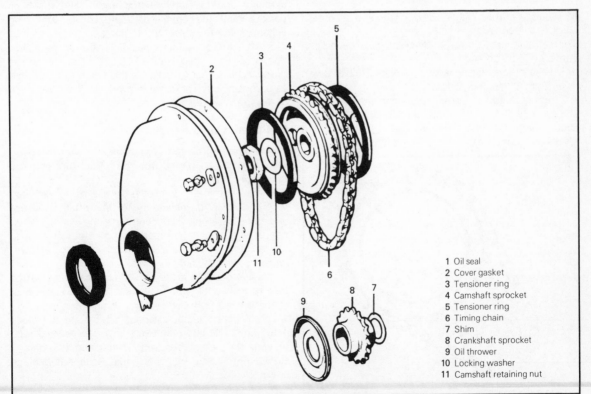

1 Oil seal
2 Cover gasket
3 Tensioner ring
4 Camshaft sprocket
5 Tensioner ring
6 Timing chain
7 Shim
8 Crankshaft sprocket
9 Oil thrower
10 Locking washer
11 Camshaft retaining nut

Fig. 9.9 The timing chain and cover

face marked F away from the crankshaft. An early type of timing chain cover and thrower must always be used together, with the concave side of the thrower facing away from the crankshaft.

9 Fit the timing chain case cover, with a new gasket, but leave the securing screws loose until the crankshaft pulley has been eased into place, thus centralising the seal on the pulley. Lubricate the hub of the pulley generously and rotate the pulley as you insert it to prevent any damage to the lip of the seal. The keyway on the pulley must line up with the Woodruff key fitted to the crankshaft before the pulley is finally tapped home. Tighten the cover setscrews evenly but do not overtighten them, owing to the risk of distorting the flange.

9.13 Removing and refitting the timing chain and sprockets

The normal reason for removing the chain and sprockets — other than during the course of a complete engine overhaul — is, of course, to replace a worn chain. If the teeth of the sprockets show a hooked formation where the chain rollers contact them, it is best to fit new sprockets also. The tension of the chain is controlled by rubber rings on the camshaft sprocket. These rings often have a fairly short life and should always be renewed when the chain and sprockets are removed for any reason.

Materials: Paraffin. Rags. New chain and also new sprockets if required.
Tools: Spanners. Sockets. Screwdrivers. Levers for sprockets. Straightedge.

1 Take off the timing chain cover and oil thrower, as described in Section 9.12.

2 Before removing the sprockets and chain, turn the engine until the dots on the sprockets are opposite each other, and on a line joining the centres of the sprockets. Check this with a straightedge. The key-

way in the crankshaft will be upright and that in the camshaft will be at approximately the one o'clock position.

3 Wedge the flywheel (if this has not already been done), unlock the camshaft chain wheel nut and remove the nut and locking washer, the tag of which locates in a keyway in the camshaft chain wheel.

4 The camshaft and crankshaft chain wheel must now be eased off, with the chain still in position, by the careful use of small levers. The sprockets can be obstinate and care must be taken not to damage their hubs.

5 As the crankshaft wheel comes away, collect the packing shims that are fitted behind it.

6 Assuming that the engine has not been rotated while the sprockets were off, the crankshaft and camshaft will be in the correct position. Fit the chain to the sprockets so that the timing marks are opposite each other and slide the wheels on to the shafts, rotating the camshaft very slightly if necessary, to line up the key with the keyway.

7 When the sprockets have been pushed on as far as possible, check the alignment of the sprockets by placing a straightedge across their teeth. If the original shims were refitted the teeth should line-up properly. If they are out of line, the chain and sprockets will wear quickly. If new sprockets have been fitted and do not line-up, measure the gap between the face of one sprocket and the straightedge and adjust the shim pack behind the crankshaft sprocket by obtaining suitable shims from your BLMC dealer.

8 After a worn chain has been replaced by a new one, it is advisable to check the ignition timing, as described in Section 12.12, as this will often be found to be out by several degrees owing to the elimination of the stretch in the old chain.

9.14 Removing the engine

The engine can be removed complete with the gearbox, or it can be parted from the clutch housing and taken out alone.

If the engine and transmission are being removed together, it will be necessary to take off the radiator and grille assembly. The engine alone can be lifted out of the engine compartment without disturbing the radiator if it is first raised and then turned at right-angles to clear the radiator grille.

It is just possible for two or three reasonably strong men to manhandle the engine out. Normally, it is best to try to hire the British Leyland engine lifting bracket, which is bolted to the cylinder head or to the block if the head has been removed. If an improvised rope or wire sling must be used, make sure that this is sufficiently strong and check that it cannot damage any auxiliaries.

Nylon-cord multiple-pulley hoists can be purchased from most accessory dealers and can handle the

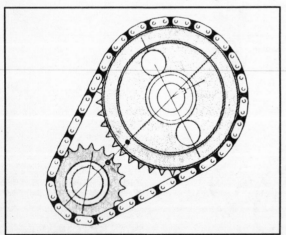

Fig. 9.10 The timing chain assembled to the sprockets, with the two marks on the sprockets opposite each other

engine safely, but be sure that the beam to which the hoist is attached is strong enough. To provide a safety factor, it should be able to support the weight of at least three men at the centre. If a suitable beam is not available or if you are working in the open it will be necessary to buy or hire a collapsible engine lifting tripod or gantry.

A final tip: the engine mounting bolts can be brutes to shift if they are rusty — as they usually are! Give them a thorough soaking with penetrating oil before beginning the work.

Materials: Any spares that are found to be needed, including new engine mountings if the car has covered a large mileage or if the mountings have softened. Paraffin. Rags. Boxes and jars for parts.

Tools: Spanners. Sockets. Pliers. Screwdrivers. Lifting bracket or sling. Jack. Axle stands. Engine lifting hoist and tripod or gantry, if needed.

To remove the engine alone —

1 Disconnect the bonnet prop and tie the bonnet fully open or remove it completely.

2 Drain the engine oil and the cooling system.

3 Disconnect the battery.

4 Disconnect the petrol feed pipe from the union on the pump. Take off the carburettor and the air cleaner.

5 Remove the top and bottom radiator hoses and disconnect the heater pipe at the front and also from the control valve on the cylinder head.

6 Take out the four setscrews and spring washers and lift out the radiator.

7 Disconnect the exhaust pipe from the manifold.

8 Disconnect all electrical connections, including the dynamo and starter leads, the high-tension and low-tension leads from the ignition coil and the oil-pressure warning light switch, plus the wire to the switch for the filter warning light, when fitted.

9 Fit the lifting tackle to the engine and take the weight. Then remove the four nuts, bolts and spring washers which attach the two front engine mounting brackets to the mounting rubbers.

10 Disconnect the clutch lever return spring from the rear engine mounting plate.

11 Place a jack under the front of the gearbox and take the weight of the gearbox before removing the set bolts and nuts which attach the clutch housing to the engine. As two of these bolts retain the starter, this must be taken off at this stage.

12 Carefully ease the engine forward to free the gearbox input shaft from the clutch hub and then lift it and turn it at right-angles to clear the radiator grille. Be very careful not to allow the weight of the engine to be carried by the gearbox shaft as this may bend the shaft or damage the clutch hub.

To remove the engine and gearbox together —

1 Carry out items 1-8 above, except for item 6.

2 Release the radiator mask by taking out the nuts, bolts and washers which retain the grille surround. The plated surround on each side of the radiator is retained by three nuts which can be reached from beneath the wing.

3 Disconnect the bonnet catch from the operating arm by removing the split pin and spring washer.

4 Disconnect the snap connectors for the sidelamp leads.

5 Lift out the radiator and the grille assembly.

6 The clutch lever return spring must now be un-hooked from the rear engine mounting plate and the clutch-operating linkage must be disconnected as described in Chapter 13.

7 Take the weight of the engine with the lifting tackle.

8 Remove the front carpet, felt and the gearbox cover plate and remove the gear lever — see Chapter 13.

9 Disconnect the engine tie-rod and the steady cable — see Sections 9.19 and 9.20.

10 Unscrew the nuts fitted with spring and flat washers which attach the rear mounting rubbers to the cross-member and then remove the four set-bolts which secure the cross-member to the frame, noting that the front bolt on the left-hand side also carries the earthing cable.

11 Carefully lower the rear of the power unit until the cross-member can be removed.

12 The four nuts, bolts and spring washers which attach the left-hand front engine mounting brackets to the tie-plate can now be removed, followed by the nuts and washers which retain the mounting rubbers on each side of the mounting plate.

13 Raise the power unit and take off the left-hand mounting bracket and rubber assembly and then move the unit sideways to clear the right-hand mounting rubber studs. The unit can then be raised and manoeuvred out of the car.

9.15 Refitting the engine, or the engine and gearbox assembly

Refitting the engine or the combined engine and gearbox is simply a reversal of the sequence followed during removal, but the following points must be watched —

1 Care must be taken, if the engine has been removed alone, not to put any strain on the gearbox primary shaft while easing the engine into place.

2 If the engine and gearbox are being installed together, it will be easier to engage the gearbox main-shaft splines with those in the propeller shaft universal joint sleeve if the car is rolled backwards as the power unit is being eased into position. Great care must be taken not to damage the splines or the oil seal in the gearbox rear extension.

3 The engine and gearbox mounting bolts should

not be fully tightened until the sling or support has been removed and the rubbers are carrying the full weight.

9.16 Dismantling the engine

Materials: Paraffin. Rags. Cleaning brushes. Boxes and tins to hold parts.

Tools: Spanners. Sockets. Pliers. Screwdrivers. Soft-faced hammer. Circlip pliers (1098 cc engine).

1 Remove the engine or the engine transmission unit from the car (Section 9.14).

2 Remove the cylinder head and manifolds (Section 9.4). Remove the gearbox, if necessary, and the clutch as described in Sections 13.3 and 13.6, Chapter 13.

3 Remove the timing chain and sprockets (Section 9.13).

4 Remove the oil pump from the flywheel-end of the engine. A new pump should be fitted on reassembly, if the engine has covered more than about 30 000 miles.

5 Remove the distributor (Chapter 12, Section 12.10). Take out the screw which secures the distributor housing to the cylinder block and withdraw the housing.

6 Screw a $\frac{5}{16}$ in. UNF bolt, approximately $3\frac{1}{2}$ in. long, into the tapped end of the distributor driving spindle and withdraw the spindle. One of the tappet cover screws can be used instead of the bolt.

7 Remove the cam followers (also known as tappets). These can be lifted out after the tappet cover has been removed, by inserting the tip of a finger in each follower. Keep the followers in the correct order and examine their working faces for any signs of pitting or cracking. Worn followers must be renewed.

8 Remove the camshaft locating plate and extract the camshaft carefully. The oil-pump drive coupling may stick to the camshaft, due to oil suction, and if this happens it must be refitted to the driveshaft with the driving lug side towards the oil pump. If the camshaft is noticeably sloppy in its bearings, fitting new liners is a job for a BLMC dealer or a specialist repairer.

9 Unscrew the connecting-rod cap bolts, remove the caps with their bearing shells, and extract the connecting-rods and pistons from the tops of the cylinder bores. Mark the connecting rods and caps on the camshaft side to ensure that they will be refitted in their original positions. Notice that the big-end bearings are offset on the connecting-rods. The rods must be fitted so that the offset sides on numbers 1 and 3 rods (counting from the timing sprocket end of the crankshaft) are towards the flywheel end of the crankshaft and numbers 2 and 4 are towards the sprocket end.

10 The gudgeon pins of the 948 cc engines are retained by clamping screws in the upper ends of the connecting rods which engage with a groove at the centre of each pin. *Never slacken or tighten these screws with the connecting rod gripped in the jaws of the vice, as there is a real risk of twisting or distorting the rod.* Fit a pad to each end of the pin, extending beyond the piston, so that the pin can be securely clamped in the vice. Short lengths of tube, or sockets from a socket-wrench set will do, but be careful that no pressure is exerted on the relatively fragile piston bosses.

11 The gudgeon pins of 1098 cc engines are a floating fit in bushes in the connecting rods and a light push fit in the piston bosses at a temperature of about 20°c (68°F). They are located by circlips at each end. After removing the circlips, scrape any carbon from the recesses in the piston bosses before pushing out the gudgeon pins. If necessary heat the pistons in hot water. If new parts are not being fitted, it is essential to keep the pins with their respective connecting rods and pistons.

12 Check the crankshaft end-play to determine whether it will be necessary to fit new thrust washers, before removing the main bearing caps and shells. Keep the caps (and shells, if new bearings are not to be fitted) in the correct order and mark each cap and its location on the crankcase to ensure correct reassembly.

13 Lift out the crankshaft and remove the remaining halves of the bearing shells and thrust washers. Inspect the main journals and crankpins on the crankshaft for wear, scores and scratches. If a micrometer is not available, have the degree of wear and ovality checked by a specialist. For notes on reconditioning see Chapter 8.

14 Thoroughly clean the crankcase, bearing shells, caps and housings and examine all the parts carefully for cracks or other damage. Normally the bearing shells and thrust washers should be renewed as a matter of course.

15 Sometimes the oil-pressure relief valve sticks in its housing. The easiest way to remove it is to insert a $\frac{1}{4}$ in. Rawlbolt into the valve and tighten the nut until the bolt has been expanded sufficiently to grip the valve. A second nut and a washer can then be fitted to the protruding end of the bolt to allow leverage to be applied to extract the valve.

9.17 Reassembling the engine

Materials: Gaskets and replacement parts as specified for a top-overhaul and for Sections 9.4-9.15. Oil and air filter elements. Replacement pistons, rings, bearing shells, thrust washers and other components as required for the stage of overhaul which is to be undertaken — see Chapter 8. Graphite assembly compound. Gasket cement.

Tools: Spanners. Pliers. Screwdrivers. Piston-ring clamp. Torque wrench. Circlip pliers (1098 cc engine).

Rebuilding the engine is simply a question of reversing the dismantling instructions, observing scrupulous

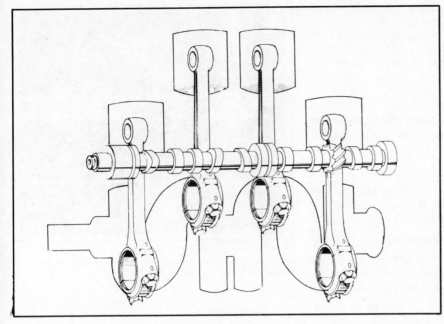

Fig. 9.11 The correct assembly of the offset connecting rods on the crankshaft journals

cleanliness at each stage. The following notes will help to ensure a first-class job. Refer also to Sections 9.7-9.11.

1 If you are fitting an intermediate engine overhaul kit, as described in Chapter 8, you will find that standard-size pistons and bearings are supplied (thus allowing the kits themselves to be standardized). The majority of engines requiring an intermediate overhaul do in fact have standard-size cylinder bores and crank-shaft journals, but if your engine has oversize bores or undersize journals, the standard parts will have to be exchanged for the appropriate sizes, so do not unpack the new parts unti the engine has been stripped and the sizes of the existing components have been checked.

2 It is possible that oversize pistons may have been fitted when the engine was new, in order to salvage parts which were slightly outside the manufacturing tolerances. So although you may know that the engine has not been rebored, or the crankshaft has not been reground, don't take the sizes for granted.

3 In production, pistons and cylinder bores are graded, and are stamped with a number inside an ellipse or a diamond. This number must be the same for the piston and the cylinder to which it is fitted. Oversize pistons are marked on the crown with the appropriate oversize, representing the bore dimension. The correct running clearance has been allowed for and the piston-ring gaps are usually correct.

4 Always use a piston-ring clamp when fitting the pistons. Lubricate the rings, tighten the clamp just sufficiently to compress the rings in the grooves and gently press or tap each piston through the clamp into the bore, using the handle of a hammer.

5 The distributor driving spindle (dealt with in item 6 in the dismantling schedule) should be replaced after the camshaft, timing sprockets and chain have been refitted and the valve timing checked, as described in Section 9.13. Screw a $\frac{5}{16}$ in. UNF bolt, or a tappet cover bolt into the threaded end of the driving spindle. Hold the spindle with the slot just below the horizontal — that is, with the larger offset flange uppermost — and slide the spindle into place. As the gear engages with the camshaft gear, the slot will rotate anti-clock-wise until its upper end is approximately at the two o'clock position. When refitting the distributor housing, use only the special bolt and washer. The head of the bolt must not protrude above the face of the housing.

6 Lubricate all parts with clean engine oil before assembly, or smear the working surfaces with graphite assembly compound, a tube of which is usually in intermediate engine overhaul kits.

7 To prevent any risk of leakage from the rear of the engine the semi-circular cork packings should be shor-tened so that when they have been pressed fully down into their grooves they protrude at each corner by about $\frac{1}{8}$ in. (3.2 mm). This will give the correct nip when the sump has been fitted, without the risk of the cork spreading sideways and preventing the sump from seating properly around the rear bearing housing. The two halves of the sump gasket must also mate snugly with the upper ends of the seals.

8 The gasket between the oil-pump body and the rear face of the cylinder block must be in perfect con-dition. This also applies to the joint between the oil-pump cover and the pump body.

9 Before fitting the gearbox mounting plate check that the soldered joint around the flange of the oil-pump protection cover is sound and that the face of the plate which mates with the block is undamaged. A new gasket must be fitted. If any oil should leak from the pump it may escape past the narrow section of the gasket and either run down the mounting plate or into the clutch housing.

10 Jointing compound should not be used on the cylinder head gasket.

11 Fit the small water by-pass hose, between the cylinder head and the water pump, before bolting down the head. It is very difficult to fit the hose once the head is in place.

12 Always use new locking washers, split-pins and tab washers. As a precaution, it is advisable to fit new big-end cap bolts and nuts. Tighten all nuts to the recommended torque figures (Chapter 17).

9.18 Renewing the flywheel starter ring

When the flywheel has been removed from the engine for any reason, carefully examine the teeth on the starter ring for wear. This is normally concentrated at two points.

To renew the ring —

1 Partly cut through the ring with a hacksaw and then split it with a sharp cold chisel.

2 Make sure that the surface of the flywheel is clean and free from burrs. Similarly check the bore of the new ring.

3 Since the ring is a shrink-fit on the flywheel, it must be heated to a temperature of 300°-400°C (572°-752°F). At this temperature the ring will assume a light-blue surface colour. If heated further, the hardness of the teeth will be affected. The easiest method of heating the ring evenly is to place it on the top shelf of an electric or gas oven, turned up to maximum heat, for at least 30 minutes. If a refrigerator is available the flywheel can be chilled while the ring is being heated.

4 Drop the hot ring over the register on the flywheel and press or tap it lightly until it is hard up against its register. The 'lead' of the teeth should be towards the register.

5 Allow the ring to cool naturally. Do not attempt to cool it by placing the assembly in water or by using wet cloths.

6 When a new ring has been fitted, it is advisable also to fit a new pinion to the starter motor.

9.19 Adjusting the engine tie-rod

The tie-rod which is fitted between the cylinder head and the engine bulkhead plays an important part in preventing clutch judder, which can be caused by movement of the engine on its mountings.

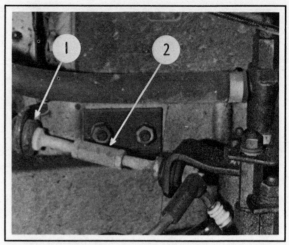

Fig. 9.12 The adjustable engine tie-rod, which prevents excessive movement of the engine on its mountings. 1, one of the rubber cushions. 2, adjustable section of the bar

To adjust the rod —

Tools: Spanners.

1 Slacken the lock-nuts on the central hexagonal section and adjust the length of the rod so that the two inner rubbers are just in contact with the brackets.

2 Tighten the outer nuts (which are self-locking) so that the outer rubbers also contact the brackets.

3 Check that the rod is neither in tension nor compression before retightening the lock-nuts on the hexagonal section.

9.20 Removing, refitting and adjusting the engine steady cable

A cable is fitted between the rear cross-member and a bracket on the left-hand side of the gearbox rear cover to prevent the engine moving forwards and to avoid any risk of the fan blades striking the radiator.

To remove, refit or adjust the cable —

Tools: Spanners.

1 To remove the cable, unscrew the nut and lock-nut at the rear end and then screw the forward end of the cable out of the bracket on the gearbox.

2 To refit and adjust the cable, screw the forward end firmly home in the gearbox bracket and then adjust the nut and lock-nut on the rear end so that the cable is just sufficiently tensioned to prevent any forward movement of the engine. If the cable is too tight, engine vibration will be transmitted into the car. When tightening the nuts, use a spanner on the flats on the rear end of the cable to prevent the cable being twisted.

10 The cooling system

A sealed, pressurized water-cooling system is used. The water — or more correctly the mixture of water and anti-freeze solution — is circulated by an engine-driven pump, passing from the engine to the radiator and back again.

A thermostat restricts the flow of water to the radiator until the engine reaches its normal running temperature, thus ensuring quicker warming-up and greater engine efficiency.

When an interior heater is fitted, some of the water is bled off to pass through the radiator in the heater, before returning to the engine.

The radiator header tank has a bayonet-action filler cap, incorporating a spring-loaded valve which opens when the pressure in the system reaches 4 lb per sq in. By keeping the coolant at above atmospheric pressure when the engine is hot, the boiling point is raised and there is less risk of a 'brew-up' on steep hills and in traffic jams.

When the engine cools down a second spring-loaded valve in the filler cap opens, preventing a vacuum being formed in the system.

The time factor

Routine jobs such as topping-up or flushing the system, checking for leaks and so on, do not call for pre-planning. Suggested times for other jobs are: Removing and refitting thermostat, 40 min; removing and refitting radiator, 1 hr; fitting a new fan belt, 30 min; adjusting fan belt tension, 15 min; fitting a new water pump, including removing and refitting the radiator, $1\frac{1}{2}$ hr.

10.1 Topping-up the system

The water level should normally be checked when the system is cold. If the engine is hot, place a cloth over the radiator filler cap and turn it *slowly* until the safety stop is reached. *Allow all steam or air pressure to escape before removing the cap.*

1 Press the cap downwards against the spring and rotate it further until it can be lifted off.

2 Top-up the header tank with a 50-50 solution of anti-freeze and water (see Section 10.3) until the level is just below the base of the filler opening.

10.2 Checking for leaks

It is often difficult to trace the source of a small leak which necessitates frequent topping-up of the expansion tank. Perished water hoses are likely culprits. Get the engine really hot and rev it up while carefully examining each hose. It is a good plan to renew the hoses and the pressure cap every two years.

Sometimes internal seepage occurs past the cylinder-head gasket. Tighten the cylinder-head nuts progressively, *using a torque wrench, to the torque quoted in Chapter 17.* If necessary, ask a garage to do this for you.

A preparation known as Bars Leaks, obtainable from garages and accessory shops, will usually cure internal seepages and external leaks very effectively. It is an inexpensive precaution to add it to the cooling water whenever the system is flushed-out and refilled.

10.3 Using anti-freeze

A first-class, fully-inhibited anti-freeze can be left in the system for two years, but it is better to drain it off each spring, flush-out the system and refill with new anti-freeze (Section 10.4), since the anti-corrosion inhibitors which are incorporated in the ethylene-glycol mixture slowly lose their effectiveness.

There will be no risk of a cracked cylinder block or a damaged radiator if an anti-freeze mixture is used in the proportions recommended in the accompanying table, but the solution will form ice crystals at low temperatures which will prevent an adequate flow through the water pump and may cause severe over-heating.

In these conditions the engine must be run at a brisk idle for at least five minutes after being started from cold, to allow the system to warm-up. To obtain complete protection at very low temperatures, equal volumes of anti-freeze and water are required. Except in arctic conditions, it will then be safe to drive the car away immediately after a cold start.

Protection given by anti-freeze mixtures

Anti-freeze (per cent in water)	Crystals begin to form		Solution is frozen solid	
	°C	°F	°C	°F
25	-13	9	-26	-15
$33\frac{1}{2}$	-19	-2	-36	-33
50	-36	-33	-48	-53

10.4 Draining, flushing and refilling the system

Two drain taps are provided. There is one on the left-hand side of the bottom tank of the radiator and a second tap at the rear of the cylinder block, also on the left-hand side. The radiator tap is not too accessible, however, and if you wish to drain the system quickly it is easier to disconnect the bottom hose.

To drain and refill the system —

1 Remove the radiator filler cap.

2 Open the drain taps, or disconnect the radiator hose, as the case may be.

3 Allow the system to drain thoroughly. If the flow is sluggish, probe the taps with a piece of wire to dislodge the sediment.

4 Preferably, flush the system by inserting a hose in the filler neck and allowing water to flow through until clean water issues from the drain points.

5 Close the taps, reconnect the bottom hose, when necessary, and refill the system slowly to prevent air locks. The safest plan is to close the heater tap and disconnect the heater hose from the tap. Insert a funnel in the hose and pour in coolant until the level is up to the top of the radiator filler neck.

6 Reconnect the heater hose, open the heater tap, fit the cap to the radiator.

7 Start the engine, bring it up to its normal working temperature, switch off and allow it to cool.

8 Re-check the level in the radiator and top-up if necessary.

10.5 Checking the thermostat

As explained earlier, the thermostat regulates the cooling-water temperature. It therefore has a vital effect on the engine efficiency and the fuel consumption. Thermostats, of course, are not infallible and if overheating occurs, or if the engine is slow to warm-up, it is logical to check this item; but remember that overheating can be caused by a number of other faults (see the chart in Chapter 5).

Many authorities recommend that the thermostat should be changed every two years, as corrosion, deposits of sludge or hard scale, or a distorted valve, can all cause sluggish action.

To check the thermostat —

1 Drain the cooling system to below the level of the thermostat.

2 Remove the securing nuts and swing the thermostat housing aside sufficiently to allow the thermostat to be extracted. The gasket should preferably be renewed.

3 If the thermostat valve is open, discard the unit and fit a replacement, which should be the correct type — see Chapter 17. If the valve is closed, place the thermostat in a pan of boiling water. If the valve does not open, the thermostat is faulty. If a kitchen thermometer is available, the opening temperature can be checked while heating up the water. Move the thermostat in the pan to ensure an accurate reading — and do not let it rest on the bottom. When a new thermostat is tested, the valve should open at the temperature given in Chapter 17. A used thermostat will give slightly less-precise control of the cooling-water temperature.

4 When refitting the thermostat, clean the joint faces of the housing and use a new gasket if there is any doubt concerning the original. If the flange of the housing is badly corroded fit a new housing. The word 'Top' stamped on the flange of the thermostat must be uppermost.

10.6 Adjusting the fan and generator driving belt

The fan belt, which also drives the dynamo, must be kept correctly tensioned. It should be possible to deflect the centre of the belt between the generator and fan pulleys by about $\frac{1}{2}$ in. (12.5 mm), using a firm thumb pressure. If the belt is too slack, it will slip; if it is too tightly adjusted, an excessive load will be placed on the water pump and generator bearings.

Fig. 10.2 Adjusting the tension of the fan belt, which also drives the dynamo. The arrows indicate the positions of the pivot bolt and clamping bolts

Fig. 10.1 Removing the thermostat from the cylinder head

Check and, if necessary, adjust the tension only when the engine is cold. It may be necessary to use careful leverage to move the dynamo, especially if the pivots and strut are binding, making it difficult to obtain sufficient tension on the belt by hand.

The belt must be kept free from grease or oil. If it develops a squeak or a whistle, dust it with French chalk or smear the edges with a little brake fluid or spray them lightly with silicone rubber lubricant from an Aerosol can.

To adjust the tension on the belt —

1 Slacken the nuts on the two mounting bolts on the generator bracket and the bolt on the adjusting strut at the pulley end of the generator.

2 Swing the generator outwards to increase the tension on the belt, or inwards to decrease it.

3 Tighten the pivot bolts and strut bolts firmly.

4 Re-check the tension on the belt.

10.7 Fitting and removing the fan belt

To remove and refit the belt —

1 Slacken the bolts in the dynamo pivots and in the adjusting strut and push the generator towards the cylinder block.

2 Remove the belt by easing it over the fan blades.

3 Refit the belt in the same way and adjust the belt tension as described in Section 10.6.

10.8 Removing the radiator

It is not necessary to take off the radiator mask before removing the radiator core but both the radiator and its mask can be removed together, if preferred, as described for engine removal in Chapter 9.

To remove the radiator alone —

1 Drain the cooling system as described in Section 10.4. Slacken the clips on the top and bottom water hoses at the radiator end and pull the hoses off the stub pipes, being careful not to strain the top and bottom tanks. Also disconnect the heater hose from the right-hand side of the radiator.

2 Unscrew the four bolts which attach the radiator assembly to the cowl and carefully lift the radiator out.

3 When refitting the radiator, take the opportunity to fit new hoses — or at least the bottom hose, which is often neglected for long periods — and refill the system with fresh water/anti-freeze solution.

10.9 Lubricating the water pump

In most cases you will find a screw plug in the upper face of the water pump, behind the fan pulley. At 12 000-mile intervals this plug must be removed and a small amount of multipurpose grease inserted with the finger. Be very sparing with the grease. Over-lubrication or the use of a grease-gun will result in the grease finding its way past the pump bearings on to the face of the carbon sealing ring, reducing the efficiency of the ring and also causing sludge if the grease mixes with the coolant. If a later type of pump has been fitted which does not have a lubrication plug, no attention is required.

10.10 Removing and refitting the water pump

While it is possible to dismantle and recondition a water pump, a new pump costs little more than the price of an overhaul kit. It is also worth remembering that replacement pumps supplied by specialist firms (Quinton Hazell, for example) are cheaper than the British Leyland pump, without in any way sacrificing quality or reliability.

To remove the pump —

1 Remove the radiator (Section 10.8).

2 Take off the dynamo.

3 Remove the fan and fan pulley.

4 Disconnect the hose from the inlet to the water pump and slacken the upper clip of the short thermostat bypass hose.

5 Take out the securing bolts and remove the pump. Tap it with a piece of wood if the joint sticks.

6 When refitting the pump, clean the mating surfaces and use a new gasket with a thin coating of jointing compound.

7 After refitting the pump, adjust the fan belt tension as described in Section 10.6.

11 The carburettor and petrol pump

The SU carburettor fitted to the Minor 1000 combines the virtues of simplicity and efficiency. Unlike some other types of carburettor, it does not contain a number of tiny jets and passages which can easily become clogged. Instead, a single large-diameter jet is used, the effective opening of which is varied by a tapered needle that is raised or lowered by a piston which rises and falls in response to changes in engine speed and throttle opening. The correct mixture strength is thus maintained under all conditions; moreover the mixture strength at any point can be altered, if necessary, simply by substituting a needle that has a different taper.

Normally, the needle that is fitted as standard, as the result of extensive tests, will give the most satisfactory results. If fuel economy *must* take precedence over performance, however, or if the car is normally operated at a high altitude, a needle that gives a weaker mixture may be justified. Conversely, when the engine is tuned for increased performance a slightly richer needle may be needed. In such cases the local Leyland dealer should be consulted. The method of changing the needle is described in Section 11.4.

The carburettors fitted to earlier and later cars operate on the same principle, the difference between the H2 and the HS2 carburettors being that a simpler jet assembly is used on the HS2 design. The jet slides in a single bearing bush and is fed with fuel through a nylon tube. This arrangement avoids the need for the cork flange and the sealing washers used on the H2 type, which are apt to leak when they become worn. The method of renewing the glands is described in Section 11.6.

Since any adjustments made at idling speeds will affect the behaviour of the carburettor right through the speed range it is not surprising that a large percentage of SU-equipped cars are operating at less than maximum efficiency, and we have therefore devoted a good deal of space to these adjustments in Section 11.3. Properly tuned, these carburettors give remarkably good fuel economy.

When such parts as the throttle spindle and bearings, piston, suction chamber and jet become worn, the carburettor can be exchanged for a new one at a reasonable cost. This may be a good investment after the car has covered, say, 40 000 miles or more.

Similarly, if the petrol pump gives trouble it is usually more satisfactory to fit a reconditioned replacement under the service-exchange scheme. Strictly speaking the pump should be tested for flow, suction and pressure after overhaul, and this calls for the use of special equipment.

The time factor

It is difficult to allot definite times for many carburettor jobs, especially when adjustment and tuning are involved. If you are a perfectionist, for example, it is quite possible to spend a morning or an afternoon on carburettor tuning. Some suggested times are: Remove and refit carburettor, 1 hr; strip, service and rebuild carburettor, 1 hr; tune the carburettor, 45 min; remove and refit the fuel pump, 30-40 min; change the air cleaner element, 15 min.

11.1 Topping-up the carburettor piston damper

There is a small hydraulic damper, consisting of a piston, fitted with a one-way valve and working in an oil-filled recess, in the suction chamber that forms the upper part of the carburettor. This prevents the carburettor piston rising too quickly when the throttle is suddenly opened, which would cause an unduly weak mixture and a 'flat spot' during acceleration. The damper also prevents the piston 'fluttering' under certain running conditions.

Never use thin machine oil or a heavy oil in the damper. Use only SAE 20 or 20W/50 engine oil. If the performance is sluggish or 'spitting back' occurs when the throttle is suddenly opened and the engine is at

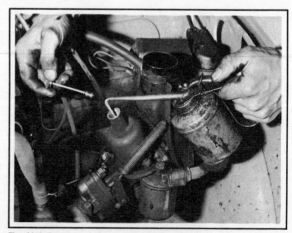

Fig. 11.1 Topping-up the carburettor damper. The combined filler cap and damper piston rod have been removed

its normal operating temperature, check that the oil-level in the dashpot is not low and that the right grade of oil has been used. Don't necessarily wait until the 3000-mile service to make this check. Sometimes the oil disappears more quickly.

To top-up the damper —

Materials: SAE 20 or SAE 20W/50 engine oil.

1 Unscrew the damper cap and remove the damper.

2 Top-up the reservoir with engine oil of the correct grade. The level should be $\frac{1}{2}$ in. (13 mm) above the top of the hollow piston rod.

3 Push the damper slowly into the recess (do not bend the rod) and screw the cap down firmly.

11.2 Servicing the carburettor air cleaner

On earlier engines an oil-bath type of cleaner is fitted, in which the air is drawn first over the surface of a shallow bath of oil in which most of the dust and dirt is trapped, and then passes upwards through a metallic-mesh filter, which is kept saturated by oil that splashes up from the bath below it. On later engines a dry, pleated-paper element is used.

The frequency with which it is necessary to inspect the air cleaner depends largely on operating conditions. Taking first the oil-bath type of filter: when the car is driven on good roads very little sludge may accumulate in the bowl of the filter over a mileage of, say, 6000 miles, but cleaning will be required at more frequent intervals if much of the driving is over the dusty, unsurfaced roads that are common in many export territories.

To service an oil-bath cleaner —

1 Remove the cleaner from the engine and dismantle it on the bench by unscrewing the central retaining bolt. If the oil in the bowl is free from sludge, it is necessary only to top it up to the level indicated by the arrow on the bowl. If the bowl is overfilled there is a risk of oil being sucked into the induction system, whereas if the level is too low the wire mesh filter will not be kept saturated with oil and will fail to trap the finer particles of dust and grit.

2 If sludge has accumulated in the bowl, wash the bowl and the filter element with paraffin.

3 Fill the bowl to the correct level with clean engine oil. The filter element will automatically be re-oiled when the engine has been running for a few minutes.

4 Make sure that the gaskets, rubber sleeve and the rubber pipe connecting the filter to the engine rocker cover are in good condition.

To renew a pleated-paper element —

1 The pleated-paper type of element should normally be cleaned at 6000-mile intervals by taking out the specially-treated paper element and removing any dust by tapping it or by brushing it lightly with a soft brush. Alternatively a garage airline can be used to blow through the element *from the inside* of the pleats. After about 12 000 miles the element should be renewed.

2 On these later cleaners it is possible to swing the air intake pipe towards the exhaust manifold, in order to improve the fuel consumption and to prevent icing-up of the carburettor during cold weather. During the summer, however, the pipe should be swung away from the manifold, to draw in cooler air. If the charge that is drawn into the engine is too hot, loss of power will occur.

11.3 Carburettor idling adjustments

The richness of the idling mixture is determined by slightly raising or lowering the jet in relation to the tapered needle, which is at its lowest point when the engine is idling. But any alteration in the height of the jet must also affect, to some extent, the mixture strength over the whole range of engine speed and throttle opening.

This is illustrated, in an exaggerated form, when the jet is lowered to well below its normal position by the mixture (choke) control to provide an abnormally-rich mixture for cold starting and to allow the car to be driven away with the engine cold. Correct adjustment is therefore important.

When the mixture control is pushed home, the jet is raised until it comes into contact with the underside of the jet-adjusting nut shown in Fig. 11.2. This nut therefore allows the slow-running mixture strength to be regulated.

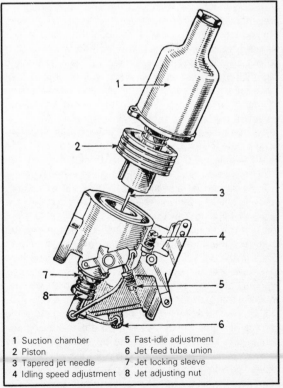

1 Suction chamber	5 Fast-idle adjustment
2 Piston	6 Jet feed tube union
3 Tapered jet needle	7 Jet locking sleeve
4 Idling speed adjustment	8 Jet adjusting nut

Fig. 11.2 The SU type HS2 carburettor fitted to later engines

The idling speed is controlled by the throttle-stop screw, or by the fast-idle screw when the mixture control is pulled out.

If smooth, stable idling cannot be obtained when the adjustments described below have been correctly carried out, hesitation or misfiring must be due to ignition faults — dirty sparking plugs, pitted or incorrectly-gapped contact-breaker points or faulty high-tension leads and insulation are likely culprits — or the trouble may lie in leaking or sticking valves, air leaks at the manifold or carburettor flange, a faulty cylinder-head gasket or general engine wear. The charts in Chapter 5 cover these and other possible faults.

To adjust the idling speed and mixture strength —

Tools: The only tools needed are a $\frac{3}{8}$ in. Whitworth spanner, or preferably an SU jet nut spanner, obtainable from accessory shops, but this is not essential; a screwdriver; and 4 BA and 5 BA spanners.

1 Lift the piston with the lifting pin, when fitted, or with the tip of the finger, and allow it to drop freely. If it does not fall on to the jet bridge with a metallic click, check for a sticking piston, an out-of-centre jet or a bent needle — see Section 11.5.

2 Top-up the piston damper — see Section 11.1.

3 Check that the throttle and mixture controls are not sticking.

4 Unscrew the fast-idle screw clear of the cam on the mixture-control linkage (Fig. 11.2 or 11.3).

5 Adjust the idling speed by turning the throttle-stop screw until the engine is running fast enough to prevent stalling when the throttle is suddenly closed. The correct speed is about 700-800 rpm, and this is usually the speed at which the ignition warning light begins to fade out. It is better to have the idling slightly on the fast side, as there will be less risk of the engine stalling in traffic or at other inconvenient moments. If it is impossible to obtain smooth idling, the mixture strength is probably incorrect.

6 Screw the jet-adjusting nut downwards, thus enriching the mixture, until the idling speed falls. The exhaust note will now have a rhythmical misfire and there may be puffs of black smoke in the exhaust gas.

7 Screw the jet-adjusting nut up, a flat at a time, pressing the jet upwards to keep it in contact with the nut and blipping the throttle once or twice to clear the rich mixture out of the engine. When the mixture is correct the engine should settle down to a smooth idle and the exhaust note should be regular. Continue to screw the nut upwards until the idling becomes irregular and the exhaust has an occasional misfire, showing that the mixture is now too weak.

8 Screw the adjusting nut down again to restore the correct mixture. Check the adjustment by raising the piston with the lifting pin or the tip of a penknife *by a very small amount* (about $\frac{1}{32}$ in., 0.8 mm). When the lifting pin is used, the initial free movement must first be taken up. If the mixture is correct, the engine speed should momentarily increase very

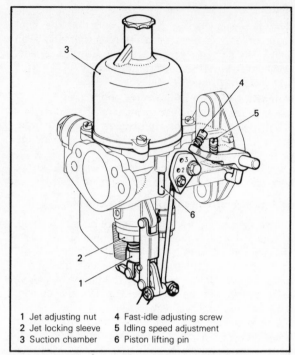

1 Jet adjusting nut   4 Fast-idle adjusting screw
2 Jet locking sleeve   5 Idling speed adjustment
3 Suction chamber   6 Piston lifting pin

Fig. 11.3 The H2 carburettor fitted to earlier engines

slightly. If the speed increases considerably, the mixture is too rich, whereas if it is too weak, the speed will decrease and the engine may stall. *Do not raise the piston too far* as this may stall the engine or cause misfiring, even if the mixture is correct.

9 If the idling speed is too high, reduce it by unscrewing the throttle-stop screw slightly. If necessary, slightly readjust the mixture strength to match the lower speed.

10 Check that there is about $\frac{1}{16}$ in. ($1\frac{1}{2}$ mm) of free movement of the mixture-control cable at the carburettor end, before the cam lever begins to move. If necessary, adjust the length of the cable by slackening the clamping bolt.

11 Adjust the fast-idle screw so that it is just clear of the cam. Start the engine and pull out the mixture control on the dashboard approximately $\frac{1}{2}$ in. (13 mm), until the linkage is just about to move the jet downwards. Adjust the fast-idle screw to give an engine speed of 1000-2000 rpm — ie., it should be running fast enough to prevent excessive misfiring due to the rich mixture when the mixture control is pulled fully out for a cold start. Push in the mixture control and make sure that a small gap still exists between the fast-idle adjusting screw and the cam.

12 Road-test the car and if necessary make any slight readjustments that may be needed.

11.4 Cleaning the suction chamber and piston or changing the jet needle.

If satisfactory idling or running cannot be obtained, the

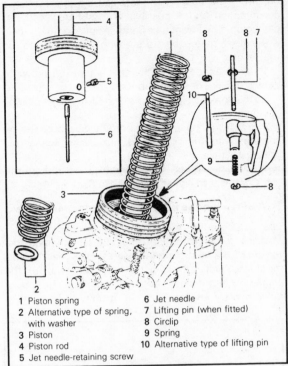

1 Piston spring
2 Alternative type of spring, with washer
3 Piston
4 Piston rod
5 Jet needle-retaining screw
6 Jet needle
7 Lifting pin (when fitted)
8 Circlip
9 Spring
10 Alternative type of lifting pin

Fig. 11.4 The HS2 carburettor with the suction chamber removed:

carburettor piston may be sticking. If it does not fall freely on to the jet bridge in the carburettor throat with a distinct metallic click when lifted and released, there may be grit or carbon on the piston and on the interior of the suction chamber, the jet may be out-of-centre or the needle may be bent. As an aid to diagnosis, make another test with the jet lowered to its fullest extent by the starting control. If the piston now falls freely, the trouble probably lies in the jet or the needle.

To service the parts —

Materials: New jet needle if required. New needle retaining screw. Petrol. Lint-free cloth.
Tools: Screwdriver. SU jet spanner or $\frac{3}{8}$ in. Whitworth spanner.

1 Withdraw the damper piston and unscrew the suction-chamber retaining screws. Lift the chamber and piston carefully, to avoid bending the jet needle.

2 Clean the interior of the suction chamber and the sliding surfaces of the piston with petrol and a lint-free cloth. Never use emery cloth or an abrasive polish. Acetone will quickly remove obstinate carbon or 'varnish' deposits. There must be a small working clearance between the piston and the chamber which provides a controlled air-leak. The parts should not be lubricated.

3 If the jet needle is to be changed, it can be removed simply by slackening the retaining screw.

4 When refitting the needle the shoulder on its shank must be flush with the face of the piston;

otherwise the needle will not be withdrawn from the jet to precisely the right extent to match any given combination of engine speed and throttle opening, and the mixture strength will be upset.

5 Don't stretch the piston-return spring. If one end has a closed coil, this should be downwards, resting on the piston.

6 Centralize the jet — see Section 11.5.

11.5 Centralizing the jet

One of the most common causes of the piston sticking is incorrect centring of the jet in respect to the needle. A surprisingly large proportion of the carburettors which are returned to the SU works as defective are found to be suffering from nothing more serious than this fault.

When the piston is at its lowest point and the jet is in its normal running position, only a very small radial clearance exists between the tapered needle and the opening in the jet. Provision is made in the jet assembly, therefore, for a limited amount of radial movement in order to allow it to be aligned with the needle. It can then be locked in position by a screwed sleeve, the hexagonal head of which can be seen at the base of the jet housing, above the spring that locks the jet adjusting nut.

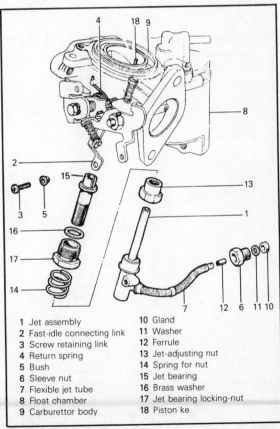

1 Jet assembly
2 Fast-idle connecting link
3 Screw retaining link
4 Return spring
5 Bush
6 Sleeve nut
7 Flexible jet tube
8 Float chamber
9 Carburettor body
10 Gland
11 Washer
12 Ferrule
13 Jet-adjusting nut
14 Spring for nut
15 Jet bearing
16 Brass washer
17 Jet bearing locking-nut
18 Piston ke

Fig. 11.5 The body of the HS2 carburettor and the float chamber

To centralize the jet on H2 and HS2 carburettors —

1 Disconnect the mixture control and the fast-idle inter-connecting link and on HS2 carburettors unscrew the union that connects the nylon feed tube to the float chamber. Pull the jet downwards.

2 Remove the jet adjusting nut and its locking spring and replace the jet, which can now be raised to a higher point than normal. Slacken off the sleeve that locks the jet bearing until it is just possible to rotate the bearing with the fingers.

3 Remove the piston damper and with a pencil apply gentle pressure to the end of the piston rod so that the needle will centralize the jet; while doing this, make sure, in the case of HS2 carburettors, that the feed tube is pointing in the correct direction, towards the union on the float chamber. Tighten the screwed sleeve.

4 Still holding the jet up as far as possible, raise the piston and check that it falls freely. If it sticks, or if it strikes the jet bridge with a sharp click only when the jet is lowered, the centralizing process must be repeated.

5 Refit the jet-adjusting nut and spring, reconnect the feed tube on an HS2 carburettor and adjust the idling mixture strength as described earlier.

11.6 Curing leakage from the jet on H-2 carburettors

When the sealing washers that surround the jet on H-2 carburettors become worn, petrol will seep or drip from the base of the jet, causing increased fuel consumption and a possible fire risk. Replacements can be obtained from a Leyland dealer and fitting them is a simple matter, best done with the carburettor on the bench.

1 Remove the suction chamber and piston and withdraw the jet, as described above.

2 Unscrew the sleeve-nut that retains the jet bearing assembly.

3 Press out the top and bottom halves of the jet bearing, with the gland washers, gland spring and sealing washers.

4 Fit the new parts and reassemble the carburettor.

5 Centralize the jet as described in Section 11.5.

11.7 Servicing the float chamber and needle valve

The SU carburettor is not very sensitive to minor changes in fuel level, but it must be remembered that the life of the float-operated needle valve that controls the flow of fuel from the petrol pump and shuts-off the supply when the petrol level in the float-chamber bowl reaches the correct height, is not unlimited. Vibration

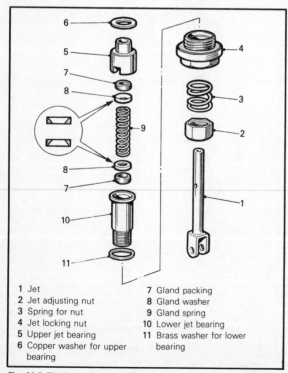

1	Jet	7	Gland packing
2	Jet adjusting nut	8	Gland washer
3	Spring for nut	9	Gland spring
4	Jet locking nut	10	Lower jet bearing
5	Upper jet bearing	11	Brass washer for lower
6	Copper washer for upper bearing		bearing

Fig. 11.6 The jet and petrol sealing components of an H2 carburettor

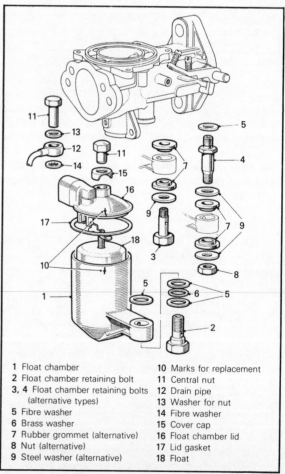

1	Float chamber	10	Marks for replacement
2	Float chamber retaining bolt	11	Central nut
3, 4	Float chamber retaining bolts (alternative types)	12	Drain pipe
		13	Washer for nut
5	Fibre washer	14	Fibre washer
6	Brass washer	15	Cover cap
7	Rubber grommet (alternative)	16	Float chamber lid
8	Nut (alternative)	17	Lid gasket
9	Steel washer (alternative)	18	Float

Fig. 11.7 The float chamber components of an H2 carburettor

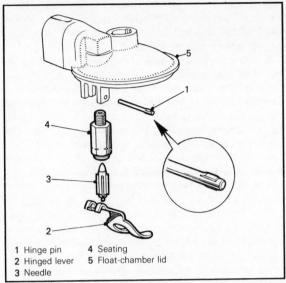

1 Hinge pin   4 Seating
2 Hinged lever 5 Float-chamber lid
3 Needle

Fig. 11.8 A typical needle-valve assembly. This is an H2 example but the HS2 differs only in detail

and movement of the valve on its seating inevitably cause wear, resulting in an over-rich mixture and flooding.

To check the valve —

Materials: New needle-valve assembly and float if required. Sealing washers. Petrol. Clean, lint-free cloth.

Tools: Screwdriver. Pliers. Spanners.

1 Remove the float-chamber lid and the float.

2 Undo the feed tube union at the base of the float chamber and swill any sediment out of the chamber.

3 Pull out the float lever pivot or float hinge pin and unscrew the needle valve from the lid of the float chamber. Swill it in petrol to remove any grit or sediment. If, after reassembling the carburettor, flooding persists, a new valve should be fitted.

4 Examine the float needle carefully for wear, which will be shown by small ridges or grooves in the seat of the needle. If there is a spring-loaded plunger on the opposite end of the needle, check that it works freely. If in doubt, renew the needle and seating.

5 When the valve is operated by a pivoted forked arm, it should be possible to slide a $\frac{5}{16}$ in. (8mm) diameter bar (such as the shank of a twist drill) between the prongs and the edge of the lid. The prongs of the lever must be slightly curved, resting squarely on the bar. The remainder of the lever must be perfectly flat and straight.

6 On a later carburettor invert the float-chamber lid and check the gap between the edge of the lid and the float. This should be about $\frac{1}{8}$ in. (3 mm). If the gap is incorrect, the metal strip, if fitted, can be carefully bent. When the float has lugs moulded on it, either the float or the needle valve, or both, must be renewed to obtain the correct gap.

The petrol pump

The SU electrical petrol pump is wired through the ignition switch and therefore operates only when the engine is switched on. The pump consists of two main assemblies. One houses an electro-magnet and carries a throw-over switch while the other houses a flexible diaphragm that forms the actual pumping medium, and the inlet and outlet valves and gauze filter.

The diaphragm, which is clamped at its edge between the two sections of the pump, forms an integral assembly with a steel armature plate that is attracted by the electro-magnet. A bronze rod, attached to the armature, passes through the centre of the magnet assembly and operates the contact-breaker at the outer end of the pump.

When the pump is first switched on, the electro-magnet attracts the armature. The diaphragm is thus pulled forward and fuel is drawn into the space behind it through the non-return inlet valve. At the same time the armature rod also moves forward and trips the throw-over mechanism in the contact-breaker, opening the contact points and cutting off the flow of current. A return spring now forces the diaphragm rearwards, expelling the fuel from the pumping chamber through the outlet valve to the carburettor. As the diaphragm reaches the end of its stroke, the armature rod again trips the throw-over mechanism, closing the contact points and supplying current to the electro-magnet, so that the sequence of events is repeated.

When the carburettor float chamber is full and the needle valve closes, the pressure developed in the pumping chamber balances that of the diaphragm return spring, so that the diaphragm remains in its forward position and the contact points remain open. The pump thus ceases to operate until fuel again begins to flow to the carburettor. It will be noticed that the pressure developed by the pump is controlled by the strength of the diaphragm return spring and is not dependent on the pumping frequency or the travel of the diaphragm.

11.8 Servicing the petrol pump

Unlike most other components of the car, an SU pump thrives best on a minimum diet as far as maintenance and adjustment are concerned. The only routine attention needed (at about 6000-mile intervals) is to remove the end cap and to clean the contact points by drawing a strip of clean paper or thin card between them, while applying light finger pressure to the outer point. If the points are badly blackened or burnt, a fine grade of sandpaper may be used, but badly burnt points are usually a sign of approaching trouble which should not be ignored. When a pump does eventually fail, it usually chooses to do so at the most inopportune moment. It is as well, therefore, to call in expert advice as soon as the warning symptoms appear.

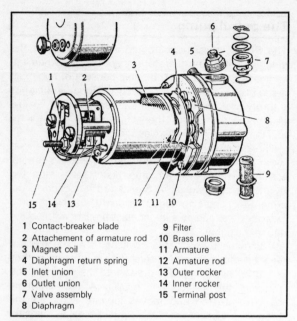

Fig. 11.9 The SU electrically-operated petrol pump

1 Contact-breaker blade	9 Filter
2 Attachement of armature rod	10 Brass rollers
3 Magnet coil	11 Armature
4 Diaphragm return spring	12 Armature rod
5 Inlet union	13 Outer rocker
6 Outlet union	14 Inner rocker
7 Valve assembly	15 Terminal post
8 Diaphragm	

11.9 Curing minor petrol-pump troubles

A pump that is basically in sound condition, however, may sometimes develop minor faults which can be cured without the need for specialized knowledge or equipment. If the pump should beat rapidly and fail to deliver fuel, for example, the trouble is most likely to be caused by air leaks on the suction side of the pump or by dirt in the valves.

1 An air leak can be cured by tightening the unions on the pipe between the pump and the fuel tank.

2 If dirt under the valves is suspected, the delivery union must be unscrewed to allow the valve cage to be lifted out for cleaning. When reassembling the valves see that the thin red fibre washer is below the valve cage and the thick orange one is above it.

3 If the pump operates slowly and becomes very hot, the filter probably requires cleaning or the pipe between the pump and the tank may be obstructed. The filter is easily removed by unscrewing the retaining cap at the bottom of the pump body. A choked pipe can usually be cleared by blowing through it from the pump end with a tyre pump. It is as well to drain the tank and flush it out at the first opportunity, to remove any accumulation of sediment.

4 If the pump fails to operate at all, first thump it with the ball of the clenched fist. This may dislodge a particle of grit. If this fails to start the pump, disconnect the supply lead from the terminal and brush it against the body of the pump. If no spark is obtained, the circuit must be traced back to the battery. If, however, current is available, it may be necessary to clean the contact points — see Section 11.8.

5 Other causes of pump failure are usually associated with the diaphragm or contact-breaker mechanism. If the diaphragm should become hardened or perforated, for example, it will be necessary to fit a replacement diaphragm and armature assembly. Sometimes the diaphragm has insufficient flexibility and restricted movement, although it is in good condition. In such cases it is necessary to dismantle the base of the pump from the magnet assembly and this work is best left to the expert. Experience has shown that whenever a pump begins to give trouble, amateur repairs seldom remain effective for very long. The best course is to replace the pump by a reconditioned unit, taking advantage of the exchange scheme that is operated by most Leyland dealers.

12 The ignition system

The ignition system shares with the carburettor the doubtful distinction of being responsible for a large percentage of roadside breakdowns, starting problems, loss of power and heavy fuel consumption. This may seem a depressing catalogue of faults — but the experience of the road patrols of the motoring associations bears it out. It is equally true to say, on the other hand, that given conscientious maintenance, there is no reason why the ignition system should not operate with entire reliability between routine services.

The system consists of a number of related components, all of which play their part in ensuring maximum efficiency.

When the engine is running, current flows from the battery through a low-voltage winding in the *ignition coil* to a pair of *contacts* in the *contact-breaker* inside the *distributor*, before returning to the battery through the metal of the engine and body.

The contact-breaker contacts — often called *'points'* — are opened and closed by a *cam* on a shaft in the distributor which is driven by the engine, interrupting the flow of current in the low-voltage winding in the ignition coil and causing a surge of high-voltage current in a *high-tension winding* in the coil. This current is carried by a *high-tension cable* to the central terminal in the moulded plastic *distributor cap*, from which it passes through a spring-loaded carbon contact to a *rotor* mounted on the top of the distributor spindle.

As the rotor turns, its tip passes close to terminals inside the distributor cap, which are connected to the *sparking-plug leads*. At the moment that the contact-breaker points open the correct plug will receive the surge of current. A spark then jumps across the *sparking-plug electrodes*, which project into the combustion chamber, firing the compressed mixture of petrol and air in the cylinder.

The time factor

None of the jobs described in the following sections is very time-consuming. For example: cleaning and gapping the sparking plugs, 30 min; cleaning and lubricating the distributor, 15 min; removing the distributor contacts, refitting and adjusting the gap, 40-50 min; removing and refitting the distributor, 25-30 min; stripping and reassembling the distributor, about 40 min; checking and adjusting the ignition timing, 20 min — but longer, of course, if a series of road tests is made as described in Section 12.13.

12.1 Cleaning and adjusting the sparking plugs

The correct type of plug is given in Chapter 17. Plugs which have similar characteristics are also available from other sparking-plug manufacturers, *but it is essential to make sure that the correct 'heat' grade is used.* Fit new plugs after 10 000 miles (16 000 km) in service.

The use of a garage plug-cleaner is the only really effective method of removing carbon and deposits from the internal surfaces and insulator. To check the sparking-plug gaps and re-set them if necessary —

Tools: Sparking plug spanner. Wire brush. Gap gauge.

1 Pull off the connectors and unscrew the plugs. Keep the spanner square to avoid cracking the external insulators.

2 Clean the points with a wire brush. If the internal insulators are dirty, or the plugs have been in service for more than 5000 miles (8000 km) have them cleaned by a garage.

3 Set the gap between the points to 0.025 in. (25 thousandths of an inch, 0.63 mm), using an inexpensive gauge and setting tool such as the Champion plug-servicing tool sold by accessory shops, and bending the *side* electrode only.

4 Clean the threaded portion of each plug with a stiff brush and smear a trace of graphite grease on the threads.

5 Blow or wipe any dust or grit out of the plug recesses in the cylinder head. Make sure that the sealing washers are in good condition and seated properly on the plugs, and screw the plugs home by turning the plug spanner *without using the tommy-bar.* Use the bar only for the final half-turn to ensure a gastight joint. Over-tightening is unnecessary and is likely to lead to trouble. If the plugs cannot be screwed in easily by hand, ask your garage to clean-up the threads in the cylinder head with a plug-thread tap.

12.2 Ignition coil and high-tension leads

The coil requires little or no attention, apart from keeping the external surface clean — particularly the moulded cap. An internal fault in the coil will show up on an electronic test set. Otherwise, the only practicable test is to substitute, temporarily, a coil that is known to be in good condition.

Test the high-tension leads between the coil and the distributor and between the distributor cap and the sparking plugs for surface cracks by doubling the cable between the fingers. Renew them if necessary. If the leads are the modern resistance type, change them after two years.

12.3 The ignition capacitor

An inefficient capacitor will cause rapid burning of the contact-breaker points and a weak spark or − if it should short-circuit internally − failure of the plugs to fire at all.

Test by substituting a new capacitor for the doubtful one, but first check for a break or short-circuit in the flexible lead that connects it to the contact-breaker terminal post − a cause of misfiring or complete cutting-out of the ignition that is often overlooked. As an insurance against future trouble, fit a new capacitor whenever the contact-breaker points are renewed. It is not an expensive item.

12.4 Lubricating the ignition distributor

Over-lubrication should be avoided. If grease or oil is thrown on to the contact points, it will become carbonized and cause misfiring.

1 Remove the moulded cap from the distributor and pull or gently prise the rotor off the end of the central shaft. Apply two drops of engine oil to the screw at the top of the shaft.

2 Smear the faces of the cam with a trace of grease.

3 Squirt a few drops of engine oil through the hole in the contact-breaker baseplate through which the distributor spindle passes.

12.5 Cleaning the distributor cap and rotor

1 Lightly scrape the contact strip on the rotor and the terminals inside the cap to expose bright metal. *Do not file them or rub them down with emery paper.*

2 Check the spring-loaded carbon contact inside the distributor cap. This sometimes sticks. Do not over-stretch the spring.

3 Wipe the interior of the cap with a cloth moistened with methylated spirits (denatured alcohol) to remove dust or oily deposits, which will provide a leakage path for the high-tension current. A cracked cap or condensed moisture on the inside or outside of the cap is a common cause of difficult starting and misfiring. An occasional spray with a water-repelling preparation such as WD40 will cure and prevent condensation troubles.

4 Examine the rotor for signs of 'tracking' in the form of dark tracks on the surface of the plastic. If tracking has occurred or if the tip of the terminal is badly burnt, fit a new rotor.

12.6 Testing the distributor cap and rotor

1 Detach two alternate sparking-plug leads, and the distributor-end of the coil high-tension lead, from the cap. Insert the end of the coil lead into each of the empty sockets in turn. Leave the remaining leads in place and connected to sparking plugs.

2 Switch on the ignition, make sure that the contact-breaker points are closed, and with the tip of a

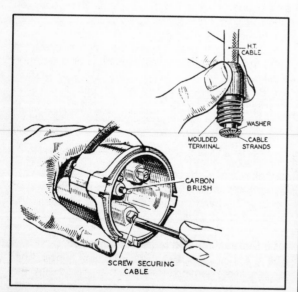

Fig. 12.1 Fitting new high-tension leads. The leads in the distributor cap are held by pointed screws. The strands of the ignition coil lead must be turned back over the washer as shown

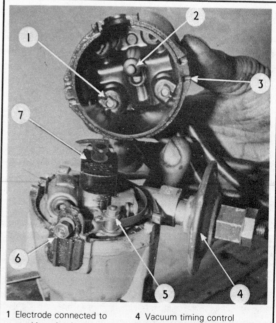

1 Electrode connected to sparking plug lead
2 Central spring-loaded brush
3 Distributor cap
4 Vacuum timing control
5 Nut securing contact spring
6 Low-tension terminal
7 Rotor

Fig. 12.2 The ignition distributor

screwdriver flick the points apart. If there has been any tracking, a spark will jump across the interior of the distributor cap.

The rotor can be checked for breakdown of the insulation as follows, without removing it from the cam spindle —

1 Remove the coil high-tension lead from the distributor cap.

2 Hold it almost in contact with the edge of the rotor blade and flick the contact-breaker points open as before. If the rotor is faulty a spark will jump the air gap between the high-tension lead and the rotor blade. Occasionally, internal leakage develops from the underside of the brass electrode of the rotor, through the plastic to the interior surface, allowing the high-tension current to jump to the cam spindle and so to earth. This can be a very elusive fault to spot but will be revealed by the above test. Fit a new rotor whenever you fit new sparking plugs and you should have no trouble.

12.7 Checking the vacuum timing control

When a vacuum-operated timing control is fitted (an example is shown in Fig. 12.3), check the following points —

1 Make sure that the suction chamber does not contain any condensed fuel. Test the action of the diaphragm by applying suction to the union. If the diaphragm appears to be faulty, fit a new unit.

3 Check the rubber connections at each end of the vacuum pipe and renew them if they have split or are a loose fit on the pipe. This is very important. Even a slight air-leak will affect the action of the control.

3 Renew the pipe if it has been kinked by careless work on the engine.

Adjustments and overhauls

12.8 Removing and refitting the contact-breaker points

Materials: Replacement contact-breaker set. Clean cloth. Petrol. Engine oil. Grease.
Tools: Screwdriver. Set of BA spanners or a small adjustable spanner. Pliers.

To remove and refit the contacts —

1 Remove the distributor cap and pull off the rotor arm. Gentle leverage may be used if the rotor is tight.

2 Unscrew the nut from the top of the terminal post on the fixed contact-breaker plate and take off the insulating bush and the lead. Make a note of the order in which the terminals and insulating bushes, and the washers on earlier distributors, are fitted.

3 Remove the screw that secures the fixed contact-breaker plate and lift off the contact-breaker assembly, or the moving arm and spring and the fixed plate, when a two-piece contact-breaker set is fitted.

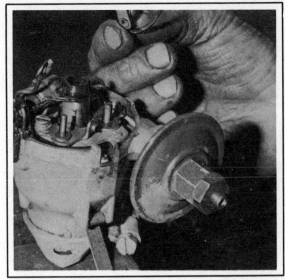

Fig. 12.3 The moving contact arm removed from the distributor

4 Before fitting a new contact set, clean the preservative off the contact points with petrol and lubricate the moving contact pivot with a trace of engine oil and the cam with a very light smear of grease.

5 When reassembling the contact-breaker set, make sure that the insulating bushes and washers are correctly fitted. The eye in the spring of the moving contact must be insulated from the baseplate, the terminal post and the securing nut. The terminal tags on the feed wire and the capacitor lead must make contact with the spring, but not with the terminal post or the securing nut. If these items are assembled incorrectly, the engine will not start.

6 Refit and adjust the contact-breaker gap as described in Section 12.9.

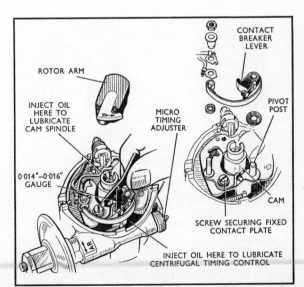

Fig. 12.4 Lubrication and servicing points on the distributor

12.9 Adjusting the contact-breaker gap

The contact-breaker gap should not be measured with a feeler gauge unless the contact faces have been trued-up to remove the pip and crater, or a new set of contacts has been installed.

When new contacts have been fitted, check the gap after they have run for about 500 miles, to allow for the initial bedding-down of the heel of the rocker arm.

Tools: Screwdriver. Feeler gauge.

1 With the distributor cap and rotor arm removed, turn the engine until the contact-breaker points are fully open, with the fibre heel of the rocker resting on the crest of one of the cams.

2 Slacken the screw that retains the fixed contact plate and move the plate until a 0.015 in. (0.4 mm) feeler gauge is a light drag fit between the points.

3 Move the plate by inserting the tip of the screwdriver in the notched hole in the fixed contact-breaker plate and gently twisting the screwdriver to open or close the gap.

4 After the securing screw has been tightened, re-check the gap and then measure the gap with the rocker on each of the other three crests of the cam in turn. If there is any marked difference in the gaps, the cam or the cam spindle bushes, or both, are worn. Stripping the distributor to carry out repairs is described in Section 12.11 but renewing the spindle bushes is a job for a British Leyland dealer.

12.10 Removing and refitting the distributor

Tools: Spanners. Scriber.

1 Remove the distributor cap and turn the engine until the rotor arm points to the position of the No. 1 cylinder plug lead segment in the distributor cap.

2 Scribe an alignment mark from the body of the distributor on to the clamp plate and a second mark from the clamp plate on to the crankcase.

3 Disconnect the vacuum advance pipe from the distributor when a vacuum control is fitted.

4 Disconnect the low-tension lead from the distributor terminal.

5 Remove the bolt or bolts securing the clamp plate and remove the distributor. Providing that the pinchbolt in the clamp plate is not loosened, the ignition timing will not be lost when the distributor is removed. However, the scribed lines are an added insurance.

6 When refitting the distributor, turn the rotor until the driving dog is felt to engage with the driving shaft. As a precaution, check the timing as described in Section 12.12, especially if new contact points have been fitted while the distributor was off the car.

12.11 Dismantling and reassembling the distributor

It should not normally be necessary to dismantle the distributor beyond the point described in this section. Further stripping is needed only to renew the distributor driving shaft and bush. Since the bush must be

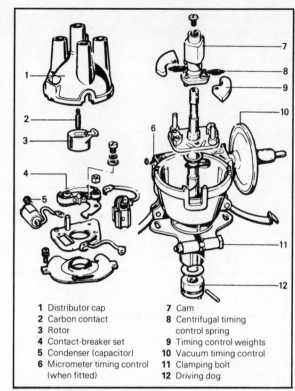

12.5 Components of the ignition distributor. In normal servicing, it is not necessary to dismantle beyond item 5 in the drawing

1 Distributor cap	7 Cam
2 Carbon contact	8 Centrifugal timing
3 Rotor	control spring
4 Contact-breaker set	9 Timing control weights
5 Condenser (capacitor)	10 Vacuum timing control
6 Micrometer timing control	11 Clamping bolt
(when fitted)	12 Driving dog

reamed, this is a job for a British Leyland dealer. In most cases, however, when there is appreciable wear in the shaft and bush, the other parts of the distributor will probably be due for renewal and the best plan is to fit a reconditioned service-exchange unit.

Materials: Any new parts required. Paraffin. Clean rags. Engine oil. Grease.
Tools: Spanners, BA and AF. Pliers. Large and small screwdrivers.

To dismantle the distributor —

1 Remove the contact-breaker assembly as described in Section 12.8.

2 Remove the capacitor.

3 Detach the link which connects the vacuum control (when fitted) to the moving plate.

4 Take out the two screws which secure the baseplate (one of which also carries the earth lead) and lift out the baseplate.

5 Turn the baseplate clockwise in relation to the moving plate of the contact-breaker to separate the two.

6 Make a note of the position of the driving slot for the rotor in the cam spindle in relation to the offset driving dog at the base of the distributor shaft, before undoing the cam-retaining screw. If this relationship is not checked, it is possible to reassemble the cam 180° away from the correct position, which will upset the timing of the engine.

7 Take out the cam-retaining screw, disconnect the toggle springs and remove the cam. Be particularly careful not to overstretch or damage the springs, which control the ignition timing when the engine is running.

8 When reassembling, make sure that the cam and the driving dog are in the correct relationship (see item 6). If one of the toggle springs appears to have a little slack, this is intentional.

9 If the vacuum control is to be renewed, remove the circlip from the end of the threaded shaft, unscrew the adjusting nut, and withdraw the unit from the distributor body. Be careful not to lose the coil spring and the small ratchet spring which are housed in the body.

12.12 Checking and adjusting the ignition timing

The static position of the contact-breaker baseplate can be varied over a small range by rotating the knurled nut on the vacuum timing control toward A to advance, and B to retard, the timing, without disturbing the main setting of the distributor. These small corrections are useful to compensate for a change in the anti-knock value of the petrol used, or variation in the engine condition.

Each of the divisions that registers with the edge of the housing represents a change in timing of 4 degrees at the crankshaft; the setting should not be altered more than, say, half a division at a time.

The initial setting — see Chapter 17 — is checked by slackening the clamping bolt beneath the distributor body and rotating the distributor in either direction, thus varying the position of the movable arm of the contact-breaker in relation to the cam: obviously, if the distributor is turned against the direction of rotation of the cam the spark will occur earlier, and vice versa. On reflection it will also be evident that altering the gap between the contact-breaker points will have a similar effect; increasing the gap will advance the ignition and decreasing it will retard. It is therefore important first to true-up the points and set the gap accurately.

Either setting is easily determined by viewing the crankshaft pulley from below. It will be seen that a notch on the rear edge of the pulley can be brought into line with one of three pointers on the timing cover. The longest pointer represents top-dead-centre, that to the right of it indicates 5 degrees before top-dead-centre and the second pointer further to the right, 10 degrees before top-dead-centre.

1 Remove all the sparking plugs except that in No. 1 cylinder (nearest the radiator) and rotate the engine until compression is felt, indicating that the piston is approaching top-dead-centre on the compression stroke. From this point, inch the starting handle slowly round until the groove on the pulley registers with the appropriate pointer. The services of an assistant make the job easier but it can be done single-handed.

2 If the distributor has been removed from the engine, slacken the clamp on the retaining plate and rotate the spindle until the rotor is pointing in the direction of the electrode in the cap that is connected to No. 1 sparking plug. The offset coupling on the distributor shaft should then engage with the corresponding drive in the crankcase when the distributor is slid into place. Check that it is fully home before tightening the securing setscrews.

3 The vacuum timing control should be towards the rear of the engine and should be vertical, with the diaphragm housing upwards. Make sure that the centrifugal advance weights are not binding and that the contact-breaker baseplate is free to rotate slightly. Set the micrometer control so that about four divisions of the scale are visible.

4 The timing can now be set by rotating the distributor body anti-clockwise until the contact points are just closed and then slowly clockwise until they just separate. If the ignition is switched on, a small spark can be seen and heard to jump across the points as they separate but a more accurate method of timing is to connect a side lamp bulb, mounted in a suitable holder, across the two low-tension terminals at the top of the ignition coil. When the points are closed the lamp will light up; at the instant that they open, it will be extinguished. When checking this point, keep a light finger pressure on the rotor in a clockwise direction to take up backlash in the drive.

12.13 Checking the timing on the road.

The static setting should be regarded only as the starting point for a series of road tests during which the timing can be precisely adjusted by the micrometer control on the distributor to suit the condition of the engine and the fuel that will normally be used. The official recommendation is that the timing should be progressively advanced until the engine just shows signs of pinking under full throttle on a moderately steep hill. While this method gives a quite good result with ordinary fuels, however, some premium fuels have such high anti-knock values that the possibility of over-advancing the engine before pinking occurs cannot be entirely ruled out.

The method favoured by tuning enthusiasts is to make a series of tests on a level road, noting carefully, by stop-watch readings, the time taken to accelerate from 20 m.p.h. to 40 m.p.h. in top gear, with the throttle fully open in each case and over the same stretch of road, so that each test is conducted under precisely similar conditions. The best ignition setting is that which results in the shortest time to accelerate over the speed range. This will also give the most economical fuel consumption.

Alternatively, start each test from a given point and note the point at which the higher speed is reached by reference to bushes by the roadside, fencing posts or similar identifying marks.

13 The transmission
Clutch, gearbox, propellor shaft, rear axle

For the benefit of the novice it should perhaps be explained that the term 'transmission', in the English rather than the American sense, applies to all the components in the drive-line between the engine and the rear wheels: the clutch, gearbox, propeller shaft and the rear axle, which includes the differential, final-drive gears and driving shafts.

It is an unfortunate fact of life that overhaul of these components, or at least the key assemblies, calls for the use of special tools and gauges and it is for this reason that it is the practice, in many garages nowadays, to fit service-exchange assemblies, rather than to carry out major repairs to worn or defective units.

As we suggest in Chapter 8, there may be little difference between the total cost of the spares needed and the price of, say, an exchange gearbox, with everything in favour of the professionally-rebuilt unit.

The time factor

Where routine maintenance jobs are concerned, the time factor must obviously depend on whether or not the work can be done quickly and conveniently with car over a pit or raised on a garage lift.

As regards more ambitious work that it likely to be tackled at home, the following are some estimated times: clutch adjustment, 15 min; overhauling the clutch-release linkage, 2 hr; fitting a new clutch driven plate and/or clutch cover assembly (including removing and refitting the gearbox), 3½ hr; removing and refitting a gearbox, 3 hr; removing and refitting the propeller shaft assembly, 1½ hr.

The clutch

The clutch is a good example of the 'repair-by-replacement' policy just described. While it is possible to dismantle the clutch cover assembly, which houses the pressure plate, thrust springs and release levers, this normally calls for the use of a press and during reassembly a special Borg and Beck gauge-plate must be used to adjust the release levers.

In any event, when a clutch has been in use for a considerable mileage it is usually found that most of the small components in the clutch cover need to be renewed and the quickest and most satisfactory course is then to fit a reconditioned assembly. This also applies to the driven plate, as it is not possible to renew the friction linings alone.

The clutch release mechanism is operated by a mechanical linkage, coupled to the clutch pedal by levers on a relay shaft. The various parts of this assembly are usually found to be badly worn when a large mileage has been covered, but fitting replacements is not a very expensive job and can easily be done at home. The work is described in Section 13.2.

The only routine maintenance needed by the clutch is occasional adjustment to maintain adequate free movement at the pedal, as described in Section 13.1.

13.1 Clutch adjustment

As the friction linings on the driven plate wear, the pressure plate moves closer to the flywheel and the clearance between the release levers and the release bearing is reduced. Eventually the levers will make permanent contact with the bearing and the clutch will begin to slip.

At the clutch pedal, the effect of this wear is revealed by a decrease in the free travel of the pedal before the resistance of the clutch springs is felt. To restore the correct clearance, which must be at least ¾ in. (19 mm) for clutches fitted to 948 cc engines or 1½ in. (38 mm) for the 1098 cc models, the length of the rod between the relay lever and the clutch-operating lever (Fig. 13.1) must be adjusted.

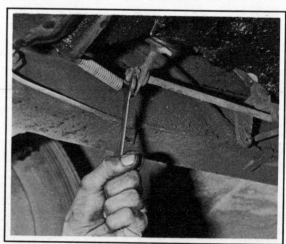

Fig. 13.1 The adjustment for free travel of the clutch pedal is at the rear of the rod shown. In the picture, the locking nut is being slackened

1 Slacken the lock-nut on the forward end of the rod shown in Fig. 13.1 and screw the adjusting nut behind the lever along the rod to give the correct free movement at the pedal — see above.

2 Tighten the lock-nut and recheck the pedal movement.

3 If the clutch does not free properly when the clutch movement is correct, or if it judders, the trouble may be caused by a fault in the clutch assembly, but first check the adjustment of the engine tie-rod and the engine steady cable as described in Sections 9.19 and 9.20 in Chapter 9.

13.2 Overhauling the clutch-release linkage

As mentioned earlier, wear can occur at a number of points on the linkage between the clutch pedal and the clutch operating lever. On earlier models the outer lever on the clutch relay shaft is coupled to the clutch pedal by a short rod. On later cars the rod is replaced by two flat links. This more robust assembly can be used on early cars if a modified clutch assembly and clutch relay shaft are fitted.

Materials: Any new parts needed to replace worn components.
Tools: Spanners. Pliers.

1 Unhook the return spring and detach the long operating rod which carries the adjusting nuts from the relay shaft by removing the split-pin.

2 Similarly disconnect the short operating rod used on earlier cars, or the pair of flat links fitted to later models. When dismantling, make a careful note of the positions of the various plain and spring washers.

3 Remove the bolts which retain the relay shaft bracket to the chassis and manoeuvre the shaft out of the gearbox housing. Also remove the retaining plate

from the gearbox housing and take out the Tufnol bush.

4 Pull the rubber and sintered-bronze bushes off the end of the shaft and then check all the parts for wear. New rubber, bronze and Tufnol bushes should be fitted as a matter of course and if the holes in the relay shaft levers are worn oval and the bearing surfaces of the rods or pins are ridged, appropriate replacements must be fitted. The bronze bush should be soaked in gear oil overnight before fitting it, or one end of the bore can be blocked with a thumb while the bore is filled with oil, then the other thumb can be used to squeeze the oil into the bush. Repeat this several times until oil seeps through to the outside of the bush.

5 After reassembling the linkage, adjust the clutch pedal movement as described in Section 13.1.

13.3 Clutch overhaul

As indicated earlier, the clutch cover assembly and the driven plate should be renewed as complete assemblies.

Although it is sometimes sufficient to renew a worn driven plate alone (if this has failed after a fairly low mileage, for example), in practice it is a worthwhile insurance against future trouble to renew both the plate and the cover assembly at the same time. It is also advisable to renew the clutch release bearing.
To remove and refit the clutch assembly —

Materials: New parts as required. Paraffin. Rags. Marking paint or scriber.
Tools: Spanners. Pliers. Screwdriver. Service tool 18G 275, desirable but not essential — see text.

1 Remove the gearbox as described in Section 13.6.

2 If the clutch cover assembly is to be refitted, mark the flange of the cover and the flywheel to ensure reassembly in the same relative positions.

3 Unscrew the cover retaining screws progressively in a diagonal sequence to release the tension of the springs without distorting the cover flange. Remove the cover and driven plate.

4 Clean the driven plate and the clutch assembly, brushing or blowing out any clutch dust from the latter, but do not swill the cover in a paraffin bath, as this will remove the essential lubricant from the cover assembly.

5 Check the driven plate for worn linings and loose or broken compression springs and worn hub splines. If oil has reached the driven plate, the rear main crankshaft bearing may be worn, but see also Chapter 9, Section 9.17, items 7-9. If the flywheel is scored, have it skimmed by a Leyland dealer or fit a new one.

6 When refitting the clutch, it is essential to centralize the hub of the driven plate, preferably by using service tool 18G 275. Alternatively, an improvised aligning tool can be made up from a length of wooden dowel, built up to the correct diameters to fit the spigot bearing in the flywheel and the bore of the

1 Gearbox drain plug
2 Later type, flat connecting links
3 Operating rod
4 Clutch-release lever

Fig. 13.2 The underside of the gearbox, showing the clutch-release linkage

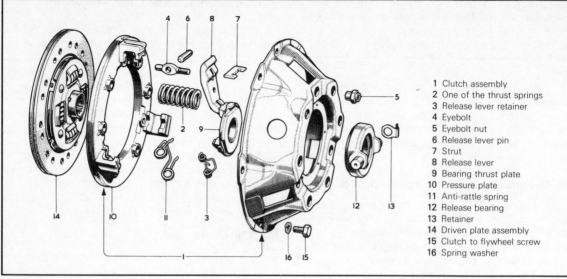

1 Clutch assembly
2 One of the thrust springs
3 Release lever retainer
4 Eyebolt
5 Eyebolt nut
6 Release lever pin
7 Strut
8 Release lever
9 Bearing thrust plate
10 Pressure plate
11 Anti-rattle spring
12 Release bearing
13 Retainer
14 Driven plate assembly
15 Clutch to flywheel screw
16 Spring washer

Fig. 13.3 The coil-spring clutch completely dismantled

clutch hub by wrapping it with insulating tape or masking tape.

7 With the aligning tool in place, and with the chamfered side of the driven plate facing outwards, refit the clutch cover assembly. Before tightening the retaining screws progressively in a diagonal sequence, make sure that everything is properly lined-up, including the alignment marks if the old cover is being refitted.

8 Refit the gearbox, as described in Section 13.6.

13.4 Renewing the clutch release bearing

When the carbon ring of the clutch release bearing is worn down, a new bearing should be fitted. It used to be said that a new ring could be installed by heating the metal cup to a cherry red before forcing the ring into position and then quenching the whole assembly in oil, but nowadays fitting a new assembly is taken for granted.

Materials and tools: as for Gearbox removal (Section 13.6).

1 Remove the gearbox — Section 13.6.

2 Remove the retainers and detach the ring from the fork.

3 Before fitting the new ring, install each retainer with its tag facing towards the side of the clutch housing, place the ring in position and push the tag on the retainer round until it locates behind the fork.

The synchromesh gearbox

The gearbox needs no attention, other than checking the oil level during routine servicing and topping-up if necessary with the grade of oil specified in Chapter 17.

Any oil leaks will be obvious while this is being done. If they are serious, ask your dealer for advice.

When trouble develops in the gearbox, considerable experience is needed to diagnose it with any degree of certainty. Excessive noise, or a tendency to jump out of gear, is usually caused by the cumulative effect of wear at a number of points, over a large mileage. Piecemeal replacements are seldom effective for very long; usually the most economical course is to fit a reconditioned gearbox, as recommended earlier.

13.5 Checking the gearbox oil level

A combined oil-level and filler plug is fitted on the left-hand side of the gearbox. This can be reached through an inspection opening in the gearbox housing which is closed by a rubber cover.

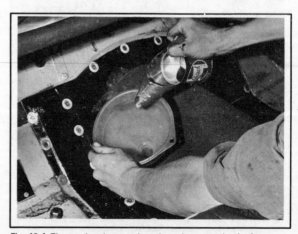

Fig. 13.4 The gearbox is topped-up through an opening in the driving compartment, after pulling back the carpet

1 With the car on a level surface, clean around the area of the plug and unscrew the plug.

2 If oil does not flow through the opening, pour in a little engine oil, using a plastic funnel, or inject the oil with an oil-can until it begins to overflow from the hole. Allow sufficient time for the surplus oil to run out before replacing the plug.

13.6 Removing and refitting the gearbox

The gearbox must be removed from beneath the car, which means that if a garage hoist or a pit is not available, it will be necessary to support the car securely on axle stands or to raise the wheels on blocks to give a comfortable working height.

The job is quite straightforward, but remember that the gearbox is a fairly heavy item and a helping hand may be welcome when removing and refitting it, to prevent any strain being placed on the input shaft which protrudes from the gearbox and on the clutch hub on which the shaft engages.

Materials: Paraffin. Rags.
Tools: Spanners. Screwdrivers. Pliers. Jack. Axle stands or wheel blocks.

1 If the car is fitted with a heater, disconnect and remove the battery to give clearance for the heater control valve when the engine is tilted downwards during removal of the gearbox. In any case, disconnect the battery.

2 Disconnect the engine tie-rod bracket from the cylinder head.

3 Remove the gear lever. Stuff clean rag into the gear lever opening in the remote control housing to avoid any risk of the anti-rattle plunger falling into the housing.

4 Disconnect the exhaust pipe from the manifold.

5 Remove all the clutch housing bolts which can be reached from inside the engine compartment — one of these secures the starter motor. Disconnect the starter motor lead.

6 Remove the carpet and unscrew the two screws on each side of the transmission tunnel which pass through the floor into the gearbox rear cross-member. The position of these can be seen from below.

7 Raise and support the car, place a jack under the engine and drain the gearbox.

8 Mark the rear propeller shaft flange and the driving flange on the rear axle to ensure reassembly in

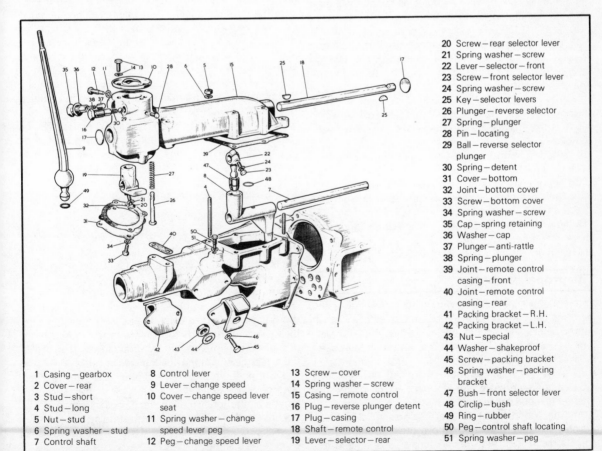

20	Screw — rear selector lever	
21	Spring washer — screw	
22	Lever — selector — front	
23	Screw — front selector lever	
24	Spring washer — screw	
25	Key — selector levers	
26	Plunger — reverse selector	
27	Spring — plunger	
28	Pin — locating	
29	Ball — reverse selector plunger	
30	Spring — detent	
31	Cover — bottom	
32	Joint — bottom cover	
33	Screw — bottom cover	
34	Spring washer — screw	
35	Cap — spring retaining	
36	Washer — cap	
37	Plunger — anti-rattle	
38	Spring — plunger	
39	Joint — remote control casing — front	
40	Joint — remote control casing — rear	
41	Packing bracket — R.H.	
42	Packing bracket — L.H.	
43	Nut — special	
44	Washer — shakeproof	
45	Screw — packing bracket	
46	Spring washer — packing bracket	
47	Bush — front selector lever	
48	Circlip — bush	
49	Ring — rubber	
50	Peg — control shaft locating	
51	Spring washer — peg	

1 Casing — gearbox	8 Control lever	13 Screw — cover
2 Cover — rear	9 Lever — change speed	14 Spring washer — screw
3 Stud — short	10 Cover — change speed lever seat	15 Casing — remote control
4 Stud — long	11 Spring washer — change speed lever peg	16 Plug — reverse plunger detent
5 Nut — stud	12 Peg — change speed lever	17 Plug — casing
6 Spring washer — stud		18 Shaft — remote control
7 Control shaft		19 Lever — selector — rear

Fig. 13.5 The components of the remote-control gear lever

their original positions, unscrew the self-locking nuts and remove the flange bolts.

9 Lower the shaft and then pull it backwards to disengage the splines at the forward end from the gearbox.

10 Disconnect the speedometer drive and also detach the earthing cable from the gearbox.

11 Unhook the clutch pedal return spring and disconnect the operating rods, or the rod and links, from the clutch relay levers. Detach the relay shaft bracket from the frame and remove the packing plate, bracket and bushes, being careful not to lose the washer fitted between the inner bush and the lever. Withdraw the shaft from the spherical bush and take off the spring. Remove the operating rod from the clutch lever. It is not necessary to disturb the adjustment.

12 Disconnect the engine steady cable from the gearbox (see Section 9.20 in Chapter 9).

13 Slacken the nuts which retain the rear mounting rubbers to the cross-member, take out the four remaining bolts which secure the cross-member to the frame (note that the forward bolt on the left-hand side is longer than the other and secures the earthing cable) and remove the cross-member.

14 Carefully jack-down the engine as far as it will go, until the heater tap contacts the edge of the battery tray.

15 Ease the gearbox rearwards until the clutch housing flange is clear of the locating dowels, taking the weight to avoid damaging the clutch hub, and then rotate the gearbox clockwise, as seen from the rear, until the flange of the housing is clear of the steering rack. The need to rotate the gearbox explains why it is first necessary to remove the cross-member completely.

16 When refitting the gearbox, again be careful not to allow the weight to hang on the input shaft. This a good opportunity to renew any worn bits and pieces in the clutch operating linkage, as described in Section 13.2.

17 When everything is back in place don't forget to check the free movement of the clutch pedal and adjust it if necessary, as described in Section 13.1.

The propeller shaft

The propeller shaft is fitted with needle-roller universal joints at each end. Each joint is fitted with a lubrication nipple and should be lubricated at 6000-mile intervals, using a grease-gun filled with multi-purpose grease. If this is done regularly, the joints should have a long life — which is more than can be said for modern so-called sealed-for-life joints which often fail after quite modest mileages.

Another good point is that — again unlike the majority of modern joints — those fitted to the Minor can be dismantled and reconditioned as described in Section 13.7 when they eventually become worn, after removing the shaft.

Fig. 13.6 It is important to keep the universal joint on the propeller shaft well lubricated

13.6 Removing and refitting the propeller shaft

Materials: Clean cloth. Paraffin.
Tools: Spanners. Scriber or marking paint. Jack. Axle stands.

1 Before disconnecting the coupling flanges, mark each flange to ensure correct reassembly. If the shaft is refitted with the joints 'out of phase' severe vibration will be set up. Similarly, if a new shaft is to be fitted, make sure that the yokes on the joints are in the same relationship to each other as those on the original shaft.

2 Have some clean cloth ready to plug the opening in the gearbox extension in order to prevent oil running out when the shaft is withdrawn.

3 When refitting the shaft, be careful not to damage the oil seal in the gearbox extension. Top-up the oil level in the box to compensate for any oil which may have run out when the shaft was withdrawn.

13.7 Servicing needle-roller joints

To overhaul a needle-roller joint —

Materials: Journal repair kit. Moly grease. Paraffin. Paraffin bath. Rags.
Tools: Spanner. Vice. Copper-faced or hide-faced hammer. Pliers. Screwdriver.

1 Remove the propeller shaft (Section 13.6).

2 To dismantle a universal joint, clean the assembly thoroughly before removing the bearing retaining clips by squeezing the ends together with thin-nosed pliers and prising them out with a screwdriver. If a clip is tight, tap the end of the bearing race inwards.

3 Support the underside of the yoke on the open jaws of a vice, with the flange clear of the jaws, and tap the flange lightly until the race begins to emerge.

4 Invert the joint, grip the protruding race in the vice and tap the underside of the yoke upwards to extract the bearing.

5 Repeat the process on the opposite bearing.

6 Rest the two exposed bearing trunnions on strips

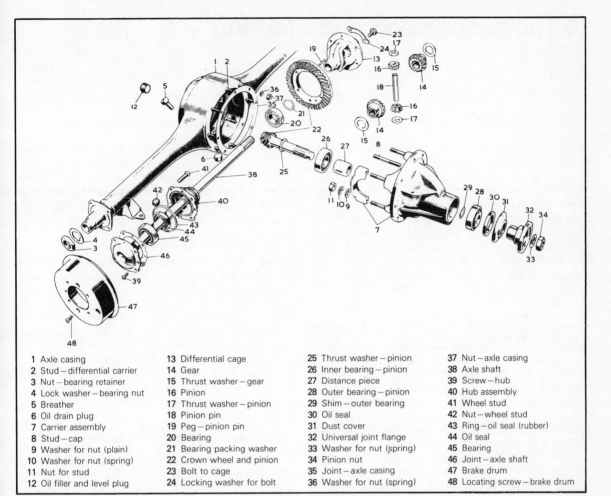

Fig. 13.7 The components of the rear axle

1 Axle casing	13 Differential cage	25 Thrust washer – pinion	37 Nut – axle casing
2 Stud – differential carrier	14 Gear	26 Inner bearing – pinion	38 Axle shaft
3 Nut – bearing retainer	15 Thrust washer – gear	27 Distance piece	39 Screw – hub
4 Lock washer – bearing nut	16 Pinion	28 Outer bearing – pinion	40 Hub assembly
5 Breather	17 Thrust washer – pinion	29 Shim – outer bearing	41 Wheel stud
6 Oil drain plug	18 Pinion pin	30 Oil seal	42 Nut – wheel stud
7 Carrier assembly	19 Peg – pinion pin	31 Dust cover	43 Ring – oil seal (rubber)
8 Stud – cap	20 Bearing	32 Universal joint flange	44 Oil seal
9 Washer for nut (plain)	21 Bearing packing washer	33 Washer for nut (spring)	45 Bearing
10 Washer for nut (spring)	22 Crown wheel and pinion	34 Pinion nut	46 Joint – axle shaft
11 Nut for stud	23 Bolt to cage	35 Joint – axle casing	47 Brake drum
12 Oil filler and level plug	24 Locking washer for bolt	36 Washer for nut (spring)	48 Locating screw – brake drum

of wood or soft metal on top of the vice, with the yoke vertical and clear of the jaws, and tap the yoke in order to extract the two remaining races, as before.

7 Wash all the components in paraffin and examine them for signs of wear or rust. A new journal repair kit can be fitted to recondition the bearing, but make sure that the races are a light driving fit in the yoke, since if they are loose, the complete assembly must be renewed.

8 Make sure that there is a complete set of rollers for each race. Smear the inner surfaces of the races, and the rollers themselves, with grease, both to lubricate them and to hold the rollers in place during assembly. Build up a ring of grease $\frac{1}{8}$ in. (3 mm) deep at the end of each race.

9 Insert the spider in the yoke and gently tap each race into position, making sure that the needle rollers do not fall out of place.

10 Fit the circlips, making sure that they are properly seated in their grooves.

11 Swivel the joint and if it is binding slightly, tap the journals of the yoke gently with a soft hammer to ease the pressure on the bearing races.

The rear axle

The teeth of the hypoid gears in the back axle are subject to very high stresses and require an 'extreme-pressure' lubricating oil of the type specified in Chapter 17, which prevents breakdown of the oil film. The oil level should be checked and topped-up at regular intervals. There is no need to drain and refill the axle – except, of course, during an overhaul.

As explained earlier, rear-axle repairs are not normally within the scope of the do-it-yourself owner.

13.8 Checking the rear axle oil level

The combined filler and level plug is in the rear face of the axle casing. A flexible extension for the oil-can or a squeeze pack filled with gear oil will make the job of topping-up much easier. The car must be on a level surface.

1 Wipe the area around the plug before unscrewing it.

2 If oil does not flow out, inject a small quantity and allow the overflow to cease before refitting the plug.

14 The suspension and steering

A glance at Trouble-shooting Chart 8 will show that the steering, roadholding and controllability of a car depend on a number of closely related factors, and it is difficult to draw a firm dividing line between some of the steering and suspension components.

In this chapter, however, we shall treat the swivel pins, their bearings, and the front and rear hubs themselves as suspension items. The rack-and-pinion steering unit, tie-rods and ball joints are covered in the sections dealing with the steering gear. This is an arbitrary division, perhaps, but it works out quite well in practice.

The time factor

Suggested times for the more important jobs are: servicing front-wheel hub bearings (one side), 40 min; adjusting height of front suspension, 2 hr; removing and refitting a torsion bar, $2\frac{1}{2}$ hr; removing and refitting a swivel pin, 2 hr; dismantling and reassembling a lower suspension arm, 30 min (plus 2 hr if the torsion bar must be removed); overhauling a lower swivel pin link, $1\frac{1}{2}$ hr; removing and refitting a rear spring, 1 hr; removing and refitting a front shock absorber, 1 hr; removing and refitting a rear shock absorber, 40 min; renewing a rear-wheel bearing and oil seal, $1\frac{1}{2}$ hr; renewing a tie-rod outer ball joint, 20 min; removing and refitting the steering rack assembly, 1 hr.

The front suspension

The front springs are in the form of torsion bars, each of which is anchored to the underframe at the rear end and attached at the front end by splines to the inner end of the lower suspension arm. The bars carry the load and absorb road shocks by twisting; as their name suggests, they are simply spring-steel rods, subjected to torsional stresses.

Each swivel-pin and stub-axle assembly, which carries the wheel hub, is located at its lower end by a screwed bush, clamped in the outer end of the lower suspension arm, and at its upper end is linked to the lever of an hydraulic shock absorber, again swivelling in a screwed bush. Fore-and-aft stresses are resisted by tie-bars, connected between the outer ends of the lower suspension arms and the underframe.

Rubber bushes and sealed, pre-lubricated joints are used wherever possible in the suspension and steering

linkage, so the only points which require routine attention are the shock absorbers (see Section 14.9), the front-wheel hub bearings and the upper and lower bearings of the stub-axle and swivel-pin assemblies — four grease nipples for the complete front suspension. These should be charged with multipurpose grease at 6000-mile intervals.

Unfortunately, if lubrication of the upper and lower swivels is neglected, the screw threads on the swivel pin and in the upper and lower links can wear badly, causing knocks and affecting the steering. Eventually the threads in the lower swivel will strip, allowing the lower suspension arm to part company with the swivel pin, resulting in the sad but not unusual spectacle of an old Minor sagging to one side with one front wheel splayed outwards at the bottom.

The moral, of course, is never to neglect the lubrication of the swivels, and to replace any parts when they become worn. We have more to say on this subject in Section 14.3.

14.1 Lubricating the front suspension swivels

The grease nipples can be reached easily by turning each wheel to full lock in the appropriate direction, but it is best to jack-up the car on the side which is being greased, to allow the lubricant to reach the bearing thrust faces which carry the weight of the car.

Even with the wheels hanging free, however, the torsion bars will still have some residual 'twist' left in them which will place a load on the threads of the bearings, so ideally the lower suspension arms should be raised by a second jack until the shock absorber lever just leaves its bottom stop.

14.2 Servicing the front-wheel hub bearings

During the 12 000 mile service each front wheel should be jacked-up in turn and the bearings should be checked for excessive end-float and for grinding or clicking noises when the wheel is spun.

If there is more than just perceptible end-float on the bearings or if the bearings are noisy, the hub must be removed in order to inspect the parts and renew any worn items. This also applies if grease has been leaking past the seal on to the brake shoes. The shoes must also be renewed if this has happened, since cleaning the linings with petrol or a grease solvent is not usually very effective.

To service the hubs —

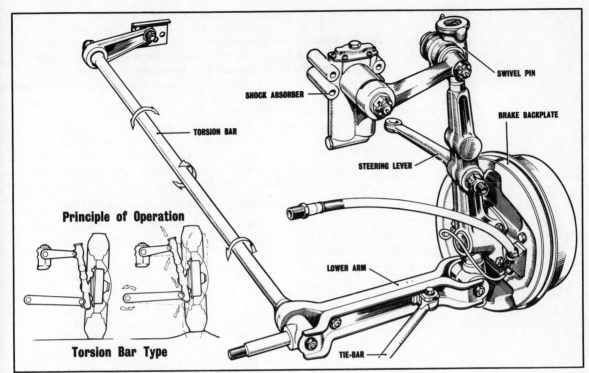

Fig. 14.1 The components of the torsion-bar front suspension

Labels in figure: SHOCK ABSORBER, TORSION BAR, SWIVEL PIN, BRAKE BACKPLATE, STEERING LEVER, LOWER ARM, TIE-BAR

Principle of Operation

Torsion Bar Type

Materials: Any new parts required. Paraffin. Rags. Multipurpose grease.

Tools: Spanners, including torque spanner. Pliers. Screwdrivers. Drift for bearings (see item 4). Jack. Axle stand.

1 Jack-up and support the side of the car and remove the wheel and brake drum as described in Chapter 15.

2 Unscrew the hub nut. *This has a left-hand thread on the left-hand side of the car and a right-hand thread on the right-hand side.*

3 Using two levers, prise the hub off the stub axle. If it sticks, tap it gently with a soft-faced mallet. If the inner bearing and grease seal remain on the stub axle, remove them with levers or a suitable puller.

4 When the bearing and seal remain in the hub, lever out the seal — it is always advisable to fit a new one — and then tap out the bearings. A narrow drift, such as an old screwdriver blade ground to the correct fit, can be inserted in the slot in the hub to remove each bearing. Remove the bearing spacer.

5 Clean the interior of the hub, the stub axle and the bearings with paraffin. Examine the hub and the axle for any signs of pitting or scoring. If this is the case new parts will be required. Check the bearing races for any corrosion, but if the bearings were sloppy or noisy when tested before dismantling, fit new ones.

6 Pack the races with multipurpose grease, working it well in.

7 Fit the new outer bearing with its broader face, on which the identification letters are stamped, facing into the hub. Half-fill the interior of the hub with grease and fit the bearing spacer.

8 Install the inner bearing, again with the broader face inwards, and then fit the oil seal with its lip facing inwards, being very careful to keep it square and not to distort it.

9 Refit the hub and tighten the retaining nut to the correct torque.

14.3 Removing the swivel pins and upper and lower suspension links

This job is quite straightforward. It is not necessary to remove the brake and hub assemblies unless a new swivel pin is to be fitted. In such a case refer to Section 14.2 for hub removal and to Chapter 15 for removing the brake drum and backplate assembly.

If the swivel pins and the upper and lower links are badly worn, new parts should be fitted. Otherwise there is a risk of the lower link pulling off the swivel pins, as described at the beginning of this chapter. If the threads are a slack fit and are causing a knock but are not too badly worn, a Leyland dealer may be able to reclaim the swivel pins by cutting an under-size thread on each end and supplying undersized upper and lower links to fit them.

To dismantle the swivel pins and links —

Materials: Any new parts found to be necessary. Paraffin. Rags. Brake fluid.

Tools: Spanners. Pliers. Screwdrivers. Hammer. Jack. Axle stands. Brake bleeding equipment.

1 Jack-up and support the side of the car and remove the wheel.

2 Place a jack beneath the rear half of the lower suspension arm and raise the torsion bar until the shock-absorber arm is just clear of the lower rubber rebound pad.

3 Disconnect the flexible brake pipe from the union and plug both openings to prevent loss of fluid and the entry of dirt or grit.

4 Disconnect the steering rack tie-rod ball joint from the steering arm, using a ball-pin extractor.

5 Disconnect the tie-bar fork from the suspension arm and remove the nuts and bolts which retain the forward part of the arm. Disengage the lower swivel

link from the suspension arm and lower the jack carefully until the twist in the torsion bar has been relieved.

6 Remove the nuts which retain the pivot-pin in the upper link and in the shock absorber arm, disconnect the link, and remove the swivel pin.

7 Unscrew the upper and lower links from the pin and if the threads are badly worn, either fit new parts or have the swivel pin reconditioned as mentioned at the beginning of this section. Also check the bushes fitted to the lower link and renew them if necessary.

8 Fit new rubber seals, since the life of the threaded pivots will be short if grease can escape or grit or water can enter the bearings.

14.4 Reassembling the swivel pin and links

When reassembling, keep the following points in mind —

1 The swivel pin fitted to the left-hand side of the

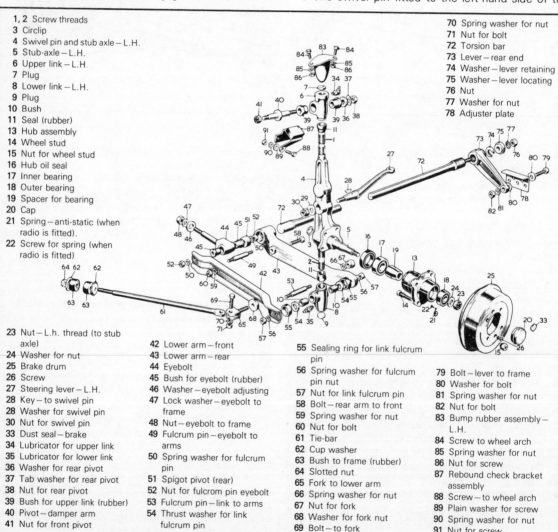

1, 2 Screw threads		70	Spring washer for nut
3 Circlip		71	Nut for bolt
4 Swivel pin and stub axle — L.H.		72	Torsion bar
5 Stub-axle — L.H.		73	Lever — rear end
6 Upper link — L.H.		74	Washer — lever retaining
7 Plug		75	Washer — lever locating
8 Lower link — L.H.		76	Nut
9 Plug		77	Washer for nut
10 Bush		78	Adjuster plate
11 Seal (rubber)			
13 Hub assembly			
14 Wheel stud			
15 Nut for wheel stud			
16 Hub oil seal			
17 Inner bearing			
18 Outer bearing			
19 Spacer for bearing			
20 Cap			
21 Spring — anti-static (when radio is fitted).			
22 Screw for spring (when radio is fitted)			

23 Nut — L.h. thread (to stub axle)	42 Lower arm — front	55 Sealing ring for link fulcrum pin	
24 Washer for nut	43 Lower arm — rear	56 Spring washer for fulcrum pin nut	79 Bolt — lever to frame
25 Brake drum	44 Eyebolt		80 Washer for bolt
26 Screw	45 Bush for eyebolt (rubber)	57 Nut for link fulcrum pin	81 Spring washer for nut
27 Steering lever — L.H.	46 Washer — eyebolt adjusting	58 Bolt — rear arm to front	82 Nut for bolt
28 Key — to swivel pin	47 Lock washer — eyebolt to frame	59 Spring washer for nut	83 Bump rubber assembly — L.H.
28 Washer for swivel pin	48 Nut — eyebolt to frame	60 Nut for bolt	84 Screw to wheel arch
30 Nut for swivel pin	49 Fulcrum pin — eyebolt to arms	61 Tie-bar	85 Spring washer for nut
33 Dust seal — brake	50 Spring washer for fulcrum pin	62 Cup washer	86 Nut for screw
34 Lubricator for upper link	51 Spigot pivot (rear)	63 Bush to frame (rubber)	87 Rebound check bracket assembly
35 Lubricator for lower link	52 Nut for fulcrom pin eyebolt	64 Slotted nut	88 Screw — to wheel arch
36 Washer for rear pivot	53 Fulcrum pin — link to arms	65 Fork to lower arm	89 Plain washer for screw
37 Tab washer for rear pivot	54 Thrust washer for link fulcrum pin	66 Spring washer for nut	90 Spring washer for nut
38 Nut for rear pivot		67 Nut for fork	91 Nut for screw
39 Bush for upper link (rubber)		68 Washer for fork nut	
40 Pivot — damper arm		69 Bolt — to fork	
41 Nut for front pivot			

Fig. 14.2 The front suspension components dismantled

car has a left-hand thread at each end and that fitted to the right-hand side has a right-hand thread.

2 Assemble a top link to the swivel pin by screwing it fully home and then unscrewing it by approximately one turn so that the lug is towards the centre of the car.

3 The tapered end of the upper pivot pin goes into the damper arm.

4 Make sure that the opening in the lug is lined-up with the groove in the swivel pin so that the bolt can be passed through. The lower link must similarly be screwed on until the groove in the pin registers with the bushed openings in the link so that the fulcrum pin can be inserted without force.

5 After assembly lubricate the upper and lower links thoroughly as described at the beginning of the chapter.

6 Top-up the brake master cylinder and bleed the brakes as described in Chapter 15.

14.5 Trimming the torsion bars

If a torsion bar on one side of the car should develop too great a permanent 'set' as it settles down in use, the riding height at the front on that side can be adjusted by 'trimming' the torsion bar. Each bar is anchored by splines at its rear end in a short arm which is attached to a frame cross-member by a bolt and a vernier plate, which allows the position of the arm to be adjusted. By altering the twist on the bar, this will raise or lower the front and the car on the side to which the bar is fitted.

Normally, this adjustment should be left to a Leyland

1 Steering lever   4 Lower suspension arm
2 Tie-bar   5 Torsion bar
3 Threaded bush   6 Rear anchorage for torsion bar

Fig. 14.3 Components of the front suspension, as seen from below. This can be compared with Fig. 14.1

dealer. If it is necessary to do the work at home, the car *must* be on a level surface and unladen.

Materials: Paraffin. Rust-releasing fluid. Rags.
Tools: Spanners. Jack. Axle stands. Wire brush. Steel measuring tape or rule.

1 Bounce the suspension up and down a few times to settle the springs and, using a steel tape, measure the distance to the ground — preferably to a horizontal flat plate on the ground — from the centre of the fulcrum pin at the inner end of the suspension arm and from the centre of the pin at the outer end of the arm. The inner end of the arm should be $1\frac{5}{8}$ in. (41.3 mm) higher than the outer end.

2 If adjustment is needed, raise and support the front of the car until the wheels are clear of the ground and remove the wheel on the side to be adjusted.

3 Place a jack beneath the outer end of the lower suspension arm and raise it until the shock-absorber arm is just clear of the lower rebound pad. *Be very careful to position the head of the jack so that there will be no risk of it slipping or toppling over when it is carrying the load of the torsion bar during subsequent dismantling.* The jack must be positioned so that the front half of the arm can be removed and the lower suspension arm fulcrum pin extracted without disturbing the jack.

4 Remove the nut and bolt which attach the tie-rod to the suspension arm and the nuts and bolts which retain the forward part of the arm.

5 Disconnect the lower swivel-pin link from the suspension arm and carefully lower the jack until the load has been takeh off the torsion bar.

6 At the rear end of the bar slacken the nut which attaches the lever to the torsion bar and remove the bolt which passes through the lever and the clamping plate. Be careful not to lose the flat washer which is fitted between the lever and the plate.

7 To raise the front of the car, select a lower hole in the adjuster plate. Each successive hole will raise the car by about $\frac{1}{4}$ in. (6.35 mm). Selecting a higher hole in the plate will, of course, lower the car to the same extent. If the vernier plate does not provide sufficient adjustment, the lever can be detached from the bar and rotated through one spline in the appropriate direction. This will raise or lower the car to the extent of $1\frac{1}{2}$ in. (38 mm).

8 Reassembling the suspension is, of course, a reversal of the dismantling sequence.

14.6 Fitting a new torsion bar

Before discussing the fitting of a new torsion bar, it must be emphasized that a bar which has already been used on one side of the car must never be transferred to the other side. The bars are, of course, interchangeable when new but become 'handed' in use and must subsequently always be fitted to the side of the car from which they were removed.

A bar must never be marked with a file or a centre-punch as this will create a stress-point which is likely to lead to the bar fracturing.

To remove and refit a bar —

Materials: Any new parts found to be necessary. Rust-releasing fluid. Paraffin.

Tools: Spanners. Pliers. Soft-faced mallet. Wire brush. Steel measuring tape or rule.

1 Carry out the preliminary dismantling covered by items 1-5 in Section 14.3.

2 Remove the nut from the rear end of the bar and slide the lever forward until it is clear of the splines. Remove the locating washer and the slotted retaining washer.

3 Withdraw the bar from the suspension arm and lift it clear.

4 When refitting the bar, or when fitting a new bar, first adjust the jack beneath the lower suspension arm until there is a difference in height of $5\frac{5}{8}$ in. (143 mm) between centres of the swivel pins at the inner and outer ends of the lower suspension arm if a used bar is being refitted, or 6 in. (152 mm) if a new bar is being installed, to allow for the small permanent 'set' which occurs when the bar is loaded.

5 Pass the rear end of the torsion bar through the lever and the cross-member. The lever is offset and must be fitted with the recessed side to the rear.

6 Fit the front end of the torsion bar into the suspension arm and slide the lever over the splines at the rear end, lining-up the end of the arm with the slot in the cross-member.

7 Fit the slotted retaining washer with the counter-sunk side towards the splines on the bar, making sure that the washer fits into the register in the lever. Fit the shouldered locating washer on to the end of the bar, checking that the smaller diameter registers with the hole in the frame. Fit the locking washer and the retaining nut.

8 The adjuster plate and the flat washer must be fitted between the rear end of the lever and the frame, aligning the appropriate hole in the adjusting plate with the bolt hole in the lever so that the locking bolt and flat washer can be inserted from the rear. Replace the spring washer and tighten the nut.

9 Reassemble the swivel link, the front half of the suspension arm and the tie-rod, lower the wheels to the ground and check the difference in the vertical height of the inner and outer suspension arm fulcrum bolts as described in Section 14.5. If necessary, adjust the torsion bar as described in that section.

The rear suspension

The design of the rear suspension is simple, orthodox and likely to be trouble-free. The rear axle is carried on semi-elliptic springs, which also locate the axle. A telescopic hydraulic shock absorber is fitted between

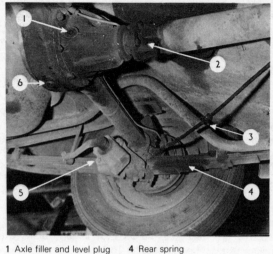

1 Axle filler and level plug	4 Rear spring
	5 Shock absorber
the axle on later models)	6 Axle drain plug
2 Universal joint	
3 Brake cable lubricator	

Fig. 14.4 The rear axle and rear suspension

each spring mounting and the underside of the body, rubber mounting bushes being used to reduce the transmission of noise and vibration.

Such a simple layout requires the minimum of routine maintenance, attention being confined to occasional checks on the condition of the rubber bushes and shock absorbers, and the tightness of the various nuts and bolts. The simplicity of the suspension does have one drawback, however, since it can allow 'axle tramp' to take place during rapid acceleration from a standstill. Torque reaction under these conditions causes each wheel to lift in succession, spin, and bounce as it returns to the road.

A more sophisticated suspension design would be needed to eliminate this trouble completely but the average owner — provided that he does not indulge too competitively in the traffic-light rat-race — is unlikely to experience tramp to any marked degree. However, forewarned is forearmed, and you should be able to recognize the symptoms if they do occur.

14.7 Removing and refitting a rear spring

As will be seen from Fig. 14.4, the rear springs and their attachments are very simple assemblies and removal and refitting is quite straightforward. For the benefit of the novice, however, the following points should be noted.

Materials: Any spares that are found to be necessary. Paraffin. Rubber lubricant (liquid soap or shock-absorber fluid — not oil or grease).

Tools: Jack. Axle stand. Second, small jack to fit beneath rear axle. Spanners. Hammer. Torque wrench. Drift. Mandrel and vice if spring eye bushes are to be renewed. Wire brush.

1 The rear of the car must be raised and supported on axle stands and a small jack must be placed beneath the rear axle to take the weight of this component and to raise it just sufficiently to place the spring in a 'neutral' position, when it will be easier to remove the shackle pins and the spring bolts.

2 Slacken off the lock-nuts on the U-bolts and remove the nuts. Raise the U-bolts until the shock absorber and bracket can be pivoted clear of the spring. Remove the plate and the rubber pad.

3 Unscrew the nuts that retain the rear shackle plates and take off the plates.

4 Unscrew the nut from the front spring anchorage bolt. The bolt has holes in its head to take a pin spanner in order to prevent it rotating but if the correct tool is not available a Mole wrench or similar tool can be used. Remove the detachable bush plates.

5 Lift the spring clear, clean it thoroughly and check for any broken leaves or a sheared dowel bolt. The latter fault is caused by loose U-bolts allowing the axle to move in relation to the spring.

6 When reassembling, fit new shackle bolts, bushes and plates if the originals are worn and also fit new rubber pads. The end of the spring which has two spring clips must be towards the front of the car and the head of the dowel bolt must register with the spring bracket on the rear axle.

7 The front anchorage bolt must be inserted from the inner side of the bracket and before tightening the pivot and shackle bolts fully the spring must be carrying its normal load. This can be achieved by placing a block beneath the centre of the spring and lowering the car until the spring is normally deflected, so that the rubber bushes will be in their normal working condition.

The rear-wheel hub bearing

The outer races of the rear-wheel bearings are located in the hubs, the inner races being mounted on the axle tube and secured by nuts and lock washers. To renew the hub bearing or the oil seal the hub must be withdrawn and this normally calls for the use of the special hub puller, which is made up from the tools 18G304, 304F and 304H. When the puller is not available, however, the hub can be removed as described below. The components of the hub are shown in Fig. 13.7, Chapter 13.

14.8 Servicing the rear-wheel hub bearings.

Materials: Any spare parts required, including a new bearing, oil seals and a new hub joint washer. Lithium-base grease. Paraffin. Rags.

Tools: Spanners. Pliers. Screwdrivers. Soft-faced mallet. Special tools 18G304, 304F, 304H (not essential). Jack. Axle stand.

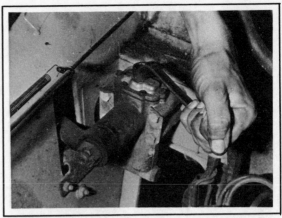

Fig. 14.5 Removing the filler plug from a front shock absorber. The tightness of the retaining bolts should also be checked when topping-up

1 Jack-up and support the rear of the car and take off the wheel and the brake drum.

2 Unscrew the countersunk screw from the flange of the axle driving shaft and withdraw the shaft by gripping the flange and if necessary tapping it gently with a soft-faced mallet. If a screwdriver is used to prise the shaft out, a new paper washer will have to be fitted when reassembling, but this is normally advisable in any case.

3 The hub retaining nut must now be unscrewed, after tapping back the locking washer. This large nut will call for a suitable box spanner (large ring spanners and sockets are apt to be expensive) but if the correct tool cannot be borrowed or hired, slacken the nut by tapping it round with a drift.

4 The special tool referred to earlier can now be used to withdraw the hub, but the simplest plan is to reverse the axle shaft, bolt it to the hub and gently rock the shaft while pulling the hub free.

5 The bearing, washers and oil seal will come off with the hub. Clean the assembly in paraffin and if a new bearing and seal are to be fitted tap the old ones out. Install the new seal carefully in the hub and tap it home with a suitable tubular drift or a socket.

6 When reassembling, check that the outer face of the bearing does not protrude beyond the face of the hub and the paper washer when the bearing has been tapped fully home. This will result in a fit which ranges from an end-float of 0.001 in. (0.025 mm) to a nip of 0.003 in. (0.076 mm) on the outer race of the bearing.

7 When refitting the hub, install a new rubber oil sealing ring in the groove and also fit a new paper washer beneath the flange of the axle shaft.

The shock absorbers

The front shock absorbers do not, of course, have an unlimited life and when they become worn they will affect the steering, road holding and the comfort of

Fig. 14.6 The rear axle and the piston-type rear shock absorber. The filler plug is shown at 1, and one of the retaining bolts at 2

the ride. After about 30 000 miles it is as well to have the shock absorbers checked by a dealer, preferably using a special test rig which enables their efficiency to be tested and recorded. Weak shock absorbers should be renewed without delay. They could cause a fatal accident.

14.9 Servicing the shock absorbers

1 The front shock absorbers form part of the front suspension linkage and it is therefore particularly important that the tightness of the bolts which attach them to the bodywork should be checked during the 6000-mile service. Although the bolts are locked by tab-washers they do tend to slacken-off, due to slight compression of the shock absorber casting, and it is usually possible to take them up by one or two flats at each service.

When the shock-absorber spindle and bush are worn, a new shock absorber must be fitted.

2 To top-up a front shock absorber, clean the top of the unit before unscrewing the filler plug and bring the level up to just below the plug hole, using Armstrong Super shock absorber oil only.

3 The rear shock absorbers can be topped-up without removing them from the car, provided that the top of each shock absorber is thoroughly cleaned before the filler plug is removed and that the greatest care is taken not to dislodge any mud or grit which could fall into the opening. The slightest particle of grit can put a shock absorber out of action, so the official recommendation that the rear shock absorbers should be unbolted from their brackets and transferred to the bench for attention has a lot to recommend it.

4 When a shock absorber has been removed from the car for any reason, keep it upright as far as

possible to prevent air entering the operating chamber and before refitting it pump the lever up and down a few times to expel any air from the cylinders.

The steering gear

The Minor 1000 rack-and-pinion steering gear seems to last almost indefinitely if it is lubricated with a grease gun filled with SAE 90EP gear oil — not grease — at 12 000-mile intervals. The lubricating nipple can be reached through a hole in the floor when the front carpet has been folded back. A maximum of five or six strokes of the gun should be sufficient, provided that the rubber bellows at each end of the rack are not leaking.

The bellows, and the gaiters which protect the outer ball joints on the tie-rods, should be inspected during routine servicing. Apart from allowing lubricant to escape, a damaged gaiter or bellows will allow water or grit to enter the joint or the steering rack, which will then have a very short life.

The inner ball joints which couple the tie-rods to the ends of the rack are protected by the bellows and lubricated by the oil which is injected into the rack assembly. The outer ball joints are lubricated during manufacture and require no attention until they eventually wear out.

Steering gear troubles

Before dealing in detail with steering-gear repairs, one or two general points must be mentioned. The most important is that many steering troubles can be attributed quite simply to incorrect wheel alignment, the wrong tyre pressures, or unbalanced front wheels and tyres. Steering alignment checks and wheel balancing must be left to a properly equipped garage. It is useless to attempt to do these jobs without the aid of specialized equipment.

Secondly, thorough lubrication of the swivel-pin links will often give a new lease of life to stiff, neglected steering gear. There have also been cases in which the steering rack has been blamed for heavy steering or knocking when the wheel is turned from lock to lock, when the trouble has been due, in fact, to the oil leaking from a torn rubber gaiter. When checking the gaiters, stretch the corrugations and look for splits at the tops and bottoms of the convolutions.

If there is evidence of oil leakage — say from a loose gaiter clip — but the gaiter itself is sound, centralize the steering rack, take off the gaiter retaining clip on the driver's side, inject not more than $\frac{1}{3}$ pint of SAE 90EP oil into the gaiter, refit the clip and turn the steering from side to side to distribute the oil in the housing.

When the steering rack-and-pinion are badly worn, the safest plan is to fit a reconditioned assembly.

A final point concerns the difficulty that is experienced in removing the tapered ball pins of the steering

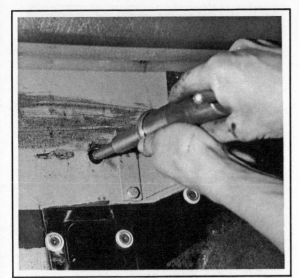

Fig. 14.7 Lubricating the steering rack and pinion. The nipple can be reached through an opening in the front floor after pulling back the carpet

ball joints from their housings. The only satisfactory method is to use a simple ball-joint extractor.

One often sees it stated that a joint can be parted by striking both sides of the housing simultaneously with heavy hammers. While this may sometimes be effective it often results only in the expenditure of a lot of hard work and lurid language, and possibly damage to the ball-pin or the seal.

The almost contemptuous ease with which a proper screw-type extractor deals with the job makes the modest cost of the tool well worthwhile. The official tool is 18G1063, but screw-operated extractors of a similar type can be obtained quite cheaply from most accessory shops.

14.10 Renewing the tie-rod outer ball joints

Materials: New joints. Paraffin. Clean rags.
Tools: Ball-pin extractor. Set of spanners. Wire brush.

1 Remove the retaining nuts and break the taper joint between the ball pin and its housing, using a special extractor — see notes above.

2 Count the number of threads showing beyond the lock-nut on the tie-rod, or paint a mark on the tie-rod registering with the face of the lock-nut, to ensure approximately correct wheel alignment on reassembly.

3 Slacken the lock-nut and unscrew the ball joint from the end of the tie-rod.

4 When refitting the joints (or fitting new ones), check that the same number of threads is showing behind each lock-nut.

5 Have the wheel alignment checked by a Leyland dealer or a garage which has precision wheel aligning equipment.

14.11 Removing the steering rack assembly

Tools: Ball-pin extractor. Set of spanners. Supports for sub-frame.

1 Remove the bolt from the split clamp at the base of the steering column which secures the column to the pinion shaft of the steering rack assembly.

2 Mark the clamp and the pinion shaft, to ensure correct reassembly.

3 Jack-up the car, place axle stands under the side members and remove the front wheels.

4 Disconnect the steering tie-rod ball joints from the steering arms on the wheel hubs — see Section 14.10.

5 Working inside the driving compartment, undo and remove the bolts of the brackets which clamp the rack housing to the toe-board.

6 Remove the rack clamping brackets.

7 Manoeuvre the rack out through the wheel-arch opening.

14.12 Refitting the steering rack

Tools: As for Section 14.11.

Reverse the instructions given for removing the rack, paying particular attention to the following points —

1 Set the front wheels in the straight-ahead position and centralize the rack by moving it from one end of its travel to the other and counting the number of turns made by the pinion shaft. Move the rack from one end of its travel by half the number of turns.

2 Line-up the assembly marks previously made on the pinion shaft and the steering column clamp and tap the splines into the clamp. Be particularly careful to make sure that the clamping bolt fits into the groove on the pinion shaft. Failure to do this might result in the column pulling off the end of the shaft, leading to complete loss of control. Also make sure that the clamping bolt is correctly positioned.

3 Tighten the bracket bolts lightly to allow the rack to swivel and align with the column. Incorrect alignment is the usual cause of stiff steering. Having checked this, tighten each nut alternately, half-a-turn at a time and check that the rack moves smoothly.

4 Have the front-wheel alignment checked by a Leyland dealer.

14.13 Wheel balancing

Wheel-wobble and quite severe vibration at about 40-60 mph and sometimes at lower speeds, can be caused by unbalanced wheels and tyres. It is advisable to have the balance checked by a properly equipped garage every 3000 miles, preferably with the aid of a dynamic balancer which allows the degree of un-balance to be checked electronically when the wheel is spun without removing it from the front hub.

The rear wheels should be balanced at the same time. They can not only cause vibration, but may also cause a rear-end steering effect if they are badly out of balance.

The tyres

Apart from incorrect steering geometry and wheel alignment, the most usual cause of excessive tyre wear is under-inflation, which also results in some deterioration in roadholding and braking. The pressures should therefore be checked at regular intervals *when the tyres are cold* — not forgetting the spare — and an accurate tyre-pressure gauge must be used. Don't rely on the gauge at a service station. More often than not these are inaccurate.

14.14 Removing and refitting tubeless tyres

Most owners will be familiar with the usual method of removing outer covers and repairing inner tubes. In the limited space available in this chapter, therefore, it is proposed to discuss only the less familiar technique that must be used with tubeless tyres.

In the tubeless tyre the inner tube is replaced by a special rubber lining which forms part of the outer cover itself and the construction of the tyre bead is modified to make an effective air seal between tyre and rim. The valve is of a normal type, but is mounted directly on the wheel rim.

When a nail or similar sharp object pierces the casing of a tubeless tyre the unstretched rubber inner lining grips the intruding nail or other sharp object closely and forms a seal around it, preventing the loss of pressure. The nail can, therefore, be left in the tyre for a short time until it is convenient to have the tyre repaired; in fact, it may not be discovered until the tyre is examined, as it should be periodically.

The only disadvantage of tubeless tyres from the owner's point of view is that it is difficult to obtain the initial seal between the beads of the tyre and the flanges of the rim. The garage method is to remove the centre from the valve and apply the airline so that the rush of air springs the beads of the tyre against the rim, providing a satisfactory air seal. The valve core is then replaced and the tyre inflated in the normal manner. A hand-pump or foot-pump, however, does not supply a sufficient volume of air to produce an effective seal.

In an emergency it may be possible to prevent leakage taking place past the beads of the tyre by wrapping a length of rope around the tread, forming a loop in it and then twisting the loop tightly with a short bar to compress the centre of the tread and force the beads outwards into contact with the rim. Vigorous use of the tyre pump should then enable the pressure to be raised to about 5-10 lb/sq in., which will be sufficient to give an initial air seal. The tourniquet can then be safely removed and the tyre inflated to well above its normal pressure — say, 50 lb/sq in. — in order to seat the beads firmly against the flanges. A

Fig. 14.8 Typical evidence of incorrect front-wheel alignment. Note the fins on the edge of the tread pattern and the 'filed' appearance of the tread

solution of soapy water should be brushed around the joint between the rim and each bead to reveal any leakage. Finally, the pressure should be reduced to the correct figure as given in Chapter 17.

14.15 Repairing punctures in tubeless tyres

It is possible to repair a normal puncture temporarily, without deflating the tyre or removing it from the rim, but all the air should not be allowed to escape from the tyre unless a garage airline or a tourniquet is available for re-inflation — see Section 14.14.

A special repair kit is used. After the pressure has been reduced to 5 lb/sq in. (the lowest pressure that will avoid the risk of disturbing the seal between the tyre beads and the rim) a tool rather like a bodkin is inserted through the puncture to free it from road grit and is then dipped in rubber solution and again inserted in the hole and withdrawn. A length of rubber of circular section is next gripped in the same tool near its end, dipped in the solution and passed through the puncture so that the end of the rubber is pushed right through the tread. The tool is then disengaged and withdrawn and the rubber plug cut off just above the surface of the tread.

If a special repair kit is not available or if the damage is more serious, the tyre should be removed by a garage and a vulcanized repair made to the inner surface.

A rubber-plug repair of the type just described must be used only as a temporary get-you-home measure, until the tyre can be removed from the wheel and a proper vulcanized repair carried out from the inside of the tyre. Although the puncture may appear to have caused only minor damage to the tread, the fabric on the inner surface may have been cut or frayed, thus dangerously weakening the tyre.

15 The braking system

The Lockheed braking system fitted to the Minor 1000 is hydraulically operated. The brake pedal moves a piston in a combined master cylinder and brake fluid reservoir (fitted beneath the floor on the right-hand side of the driving compartment), generating pressure in the fluid which is transmitted through pipelines to small pistons, working in cylinders attached to the brake backplates. As each piston moves outwards, it forces one end of the brake shoe against the rotating drum.

Two operating pistons are fitted to each front brake, and a single piston operates both shoes in each rear brake. The rear brake pistons can also be moved outwards mechanically, by leverage applied to short levers coupled by cables to the handbrake, thus providing an effective parking brake and also a modest second line of defence in the event of the hydraulic system failing.

The pressure generated in the master cylinder is transmitted equally thoughout the system, thus providing balanced braking — but this is true only up to a point as the front brakes are more powerful than the rear, two pistons being fitted to each brake and providing what is termed a 'two-leading-shoe' effect. This arrangement compensates for the extra weight that is thrown on to the front wheels when the car is braked, reducing the adhesion of the rear tyres and improving that of the front.

If the friction of one or more of the brake linings is reduced by oil or grease, however — as the result, for example, of a defective hub oil seal — unbalanced braking is bound to result.

Practical pointers

As with other components of the car, 'repair by replacement' is assuming increasing importance where braking systems are concerned. Service-exchange sets or relined brake shoes from a reputable supplier are a better proposition than attempting to reline existing shoes. Similarly, it is preferable to fit new master and slave cylinders instead of installing new rubber seals in the old components. Brake manufacturers, in fact, tend increasingly to supply only new or reconditioned assemblies, instead of repair kits.

These considerations will explain why we have not included in this chapter detailed instructions for stripping or repairing units concerned.

When dealing with brake fluid remember that it acts as a very efficient paint stripper — so be sure to keep it away from the bodywork. Any drips or splashes should be wiped off immediately and the area washed with water and detergent.

The time factor

A complete check on the braking system can be carried out comfortably in a morning. Typical times for other individual jobs are: Fitting new brake shoes to two drum brakes, bleeding brakes, 45 min; adjusting brakes, 20 min; per brake.

Routine servicing

15.1 Topping-up the brake fluid reservoir

This is largely a precautionary check. If frequent topping-up is needed, look for fluid leakage from the pipelines, unions or hydraulic cylinders. Since brake fluid specifications change from time to time (to take advantage of improved technology), ask your British Leyland dealer for the correct grade for your car.

Materials: Correct grade of Lockheed brake fluid. Methylated spirits. Clean rag, free from fluff.

1 The filler plug (Fig. 15.1) will be seen when the carpet in front of the driving seat is turned back. Brush away all grit before unscrewing it; if grit should fall into the master cylinder it can cause serious trouble.

2 Top-up the fluid to within $\frac{1}{4}$ in. (6 mm) below the threads of the filler plug.

3 Clean the inside of the filler plug and check that the air vent hole is not clogged.

4 If the fluid level has fallen noticeably, ask an assistant to depress the brake pedal firmly while you check all the unions and pipelines for any sign of leakage.

15.2 Changing the brake fluid

Brake fluid absorbs moisture from the air through the vent hole in the reservoir filler plug. Some moisture can also be drawn in past the wheel-cylinder seals. Since this moisture seriously lowers the boiling point of the fluid, 'brake fade', or complete brake failure, can result when the fluid boils in the wheel cylinders under heavy or prolonged braking conditions. The diagnosis is confirmed if normal braking is restored when the brakes cool down. The water in the fluid also corrodes the internal parts of the hydraulic components. The fluid should therefore be changed after 24 000 miles, or two years, in service.

Obviously, fluid should never be stored in an unsealed container, and old fluid that has been bled from the system must not be re-used.

Materials and Tools: As for bleeding the brakes — see Section 15.3.

Fig. 15.1 The filler plug for the brake fluid reservoir is beneath the front carpet

The fluid is changed by opening the bleed screw on each wheel cylinder in turn, fitting a tube to the nipple, with its lower end in a suitable container, and pumping the brake pedal to expel the old fluid. The process is the same as for bleeding the brakes (Section 15.3) but all the fluid in the system is pumped out and replaced by new fluid.

15.3 Bleeding the brakes

This is *not* a routine job. It should be necessary to expel air from the system only if any of the unions have been undone or new parts have been fitted, but air can be drawn in past worn wheel-cylinder or master-cylinder seals — in which case renewal of the parts is obviously indicated.

The brake-bleeding procedure is the same as for changing the fluid, but it is necessary only to pump the pedal until air bubbles no longer issue from the bleed pipe. The reservoir must be topped-up at frequent intervals to prevent air entering the system.

Materials: Tin of correct grade of brake fluid.

Tools: Brake bleed valve spanner. Length of rubber or plastic tube to fit bleed nipple. Container for fluid bled from system. There are also a number of 'easy bleeding' devices, obtainable from accessory shops, which make brake-bleeding a simple, one-man operation.

1 There are two bleed valves on the backplate of each front brake and one on each rear brake. Attach a rubber or transparent plastic tube to one of these nipples, passing it through a box spanner that fits the hexagon on the nipple, and submerge the free end of the tube in a little brake fluid in a clean glass jar.

2 Open the bleed valve one full turn.

3 While an assistant pumps the brake pedal with slow, full strokes, watch the fluid which flows from the bleed tube and top-up the reservoir as the level falls.

4 When clean fluid, free from bubbles, issues from the tube, close the bleed screw while the pedal is held down.

5 Repeat the process at the other wheel cylinders. The best sequence is: left-hand front brake; right-hand front; left-hand rear; right-hand rear.

15.4 Adjusting the brakes

When pedal travel becomes excessive the brake shoes must be adjusted to compensate for wear of the friction linings.

Before beginning work, first make sure that the tyres are inflated to the correct pressure and that the front wheel bearings do not have excessive bearing 'play'.

Tools: Jack. Screwdriver. Wheel-nut spanner.

1 Jack-up the car to allow each wheel to be adjusted in turn and ensure that the wheel rotates freely. The handbrake, of course, should be in the fully-released position when adjusting the rear brakes, at least one other wheel being securely chocked to prevent movement.

2 There are two slotted, self-locking adjusters in each front brake and one in each rear drum, which can be rotated by passing a screwdriver through holes in the drums. On the earlier Minors holes were also provided in the wheel beneath the nave plate, and it was unnecessary to remove the wheel when carrying out the adjustment. The strengthened wheels fitted to the Minor 1000 (and also supplied as spares for earlier models), however, do not have these access holes. It is therefore necessary to remove the wheel and also the rubber plugs that seal the openings in the drum against the entry of dust or moisture, but before doing so, spin the wheel and apply the brake pedal hard to centralize the expanders.

3 If the rubber seals are missing, replacements should be obtained as soon as possible. Make sure that they are of the correct type for the later pattern of wheel, as the original type of seal will prevent the modified wheel from fitting squarely against the brake drum.

Fig. 15.2 A front brake with the drum removed. The arrows indicate the adjusting screws

Fig. 15.3 Adjusting a front brake. A second adjuster is also fitted — see Fig. 15.2.

4 The position of the adjusters in the front brakes can be seen from Fig. 15.2. The single adjuster in each rear brake can be found by bringing the hole in the drum to approximately the '5 o'clock' or '7 o'clock' position. A torch or an inspection lamp is useful when locating the adjusters or a mirror may be used to reflect the light through the hole in the drum.

5 Tighten each adjuster by turning the screw clockwise until the shoe is locked on the drum and slacken back the adjuster one 'click' until the wheel rotates freely.

6 Test the brakes on a dry road, preferably uncambered. Apply the brakes hard at about 30 mph and examine the braking marks to determine whether any wheel is locking before the remainder. It should also be noted whether there is a tendency to pull towards one side of the road.

7 If the brakes are inefficient or unbalanced, the cause is most probably grease on the linings. The use of correct front wheel bearing lubricant and care not to overfill the back axle, as well as replacing grease retainers when leakage is indicated, will help to maintain braking efficiency. If the linings are badly saturated with grease or oil, new, relined brake shoes should be fitted, as described in Section 15.7.

15.5 Handbrake adjustment

Normally, adjustment at the rear-brake wheel cylinders will automatically take up any excessive free movement on the handbrake lever. In time, however, the handbrake cable will stretch. It is then necessary to take up the slack by means of the two adjusting nuts at the base of the handbrake lever.

If the handbrake does not begin to grip when it is pulled on to the extent of five clicks of the ratchet and it has been checked that the brake linings are in good condition and that the shoe adjustments are correct, adjust the cables as follows —

Tools: Spanner. Jack. Axle stands.

1 Raise and support the rear of the car so that both rear wheels are clear of the ground.

2 Pull up the handbrake to the extent of five clicks and adjust the nut on each cable until it is just possible to rotate each wheel by applying a heavy pull. The resistance at each wheel must, of course, be equal. The handbrake should then be fully released and it should be checked that both brakes are completely free.

3 Any tendency of the rear brakes to remain on will probably be caused by the brake cables binding in their conduits. Generous lubrication of the cables through the nipples provided should prevent this trouble. There is a lot to be said for using graphited grease at these points.

15.6 Servicing a drum brake

A drum brake service consists of removing the brake drums, cleaning out accumulations of brake dust and road grit, checking the operating cylinders and adjusters for binding and the cylinder seals for fluid leakage, and renewing the brake shoes if there appears to be any risk of the brake linings wearing down flush with the rivets before the next service is carried out. Special points to look for are seizure of the adjusting screws, seizing of the pistons in the cylinders and binding of the handbrake operating mechanism. These faults are very common on older cars.

Materials: Paraffin. Methylated spirits. Penetrating oil or rust-releasing fluid. Clean rags. Anti-seize lubricant, such as Shell Polybutylcuprysil (PBC) grease, SB2628. For a complete overhaul: Replacement relined brake shoes. Set of new pull-off springs. Possibly, new wheel cylinders.

Tools: Screwdriver. Pliers. Hammer, preferably copper or hide-faced.

1 After jacking-up the car and removing the wheel, slacken off the adjuster, or the two adjusters, as the case may be, as far as possible. The drum can then be drawn off after the two countersunk securing screws have been removed.

2 Withdraw the clevis pin to release the handbrake operating lever from the cable.

3 Brush out all brake dust and grit from inside the drum and from the components mounted on the backplate. *Be careful not to inhale the dust*.

4 Peel back the rubber seal on each operating cylinder and check for any leakage of fluid past the piston. If leakage has occurred, the operating cylinder should be renewed, as described later in this section.

5 If the brake linings have not worn down so that the rivets are near the surface, and the drums are not badly scored (light scoring is inevitable) the brake is fit for a further period of service, until the next routine inspection becomes due. Otherwise, continue the stripping as follows —

6 Make a careful note of the positions of the two springs (which are of different types) in relation to the shoes. It is wisest to work on only one brake at a time so that the other brake will be available for reference if difficulties are encountered during reassembly.

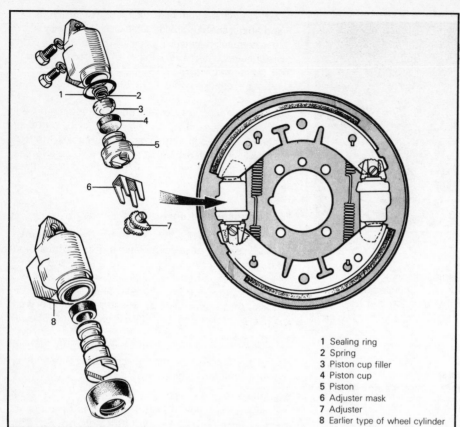

1 Sealing ring
2 Spring
3 Piston cup filler
4 Piston cup
5 Piston
6 Adjuster mask
7 Adjuster
8 Earlier type of wheel cylinder

Fig. 15.4
A two-leading-shoe front brake. The later type of wheel cylinder is shown top left, and the earlier type below it

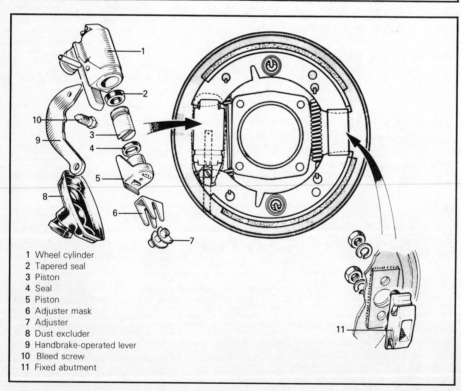

1 Wheel cylinder
2 Tapered seal
3 Piston
4 Seal
5 Piston
6 Adjuster mask
7 Adjuster
8 Dust excluder
9 Handbrake-operated lever
10 Bleed screw
11 Fixed abutment

Fig. 15.5 A typical rear brake assembly. Early models differ in detail but are basically similar

7 The shoes and pull-off springs are more accessible if the hubs are removed, but this may call for the use of a special hub withdrawal tool, as described in Chapter 14. In practice, it is usually possible to remove the shoes with the hubs in place by first withdrawing the steady springs from the centre of the web of each shoe (when fitted), pressing them inwards and turning them to disengage them, and then levering the tip of each shoe out of the adjuster fork. The shoes can then be collapsed together, allowing the pull-off springs to be unhooked and the shoes removed.

8 If no further dismantling is required, check that neither of the pistons is seized in its bore. Then tighten a loop of wire or string across the ends of the pistons to prevent them being ejected from the cylinders.

9 If a piston has seized, remove the wheel cylinder after disconnecting the fluid pipeline. Plug the pipe to prevent fluid being lost and dirt entering the pipeline.

10 If it is intended to fit new rubber seals to the pistons, pull each piston out of its bore, clean the interior of the cylinder with methylated spirits and if there is the slightest sign of pitting or scoring, reject it. *If the bore is in perfect condition,* fit a new cup and dust seal, following the instructions included with the repair kit.

15.7 Reassembling a drum brake.

Materials and tools: As for Section 15.6. If a wheel cylinder has been removed and refitted, brake bleeding equipment (Section 15.3) will also be needed.

1 Carefully inspect the brake shoes and renew them if they are worn down so that the rivet heads are nearly flush with the surface, or if the linings have been contaminated by oil or hydraulic fluid.

2 Preferably fit new pull-off springs. If doubtful, compare one of the old springs with a new spring.

3 Clean down the backplates with paraffin, but keep this away from the operating cylinders and rubber dust seals. Wipe the inside of the drum and the friction linings with methylated spirits.

4 Lubricate the various rubbing surfaces of the shoes and expanders with special high-melting-point brake grease, but keep the grease away from the linings, rubber parts and the interior of the drum.

5 Refit the shoes, reversing the sequence followed during dismantling. The trailing shoe in a rear brake has a rectangular boss at one end of the web and must be fitted in the upper position, with the boss at the cylinder end of the shoe. The leading shoe — the lower one — has a recessed end which must be engaged with the shoe adjuster on the wheel cylinder. The longer spring must be fitted between the cylinder ends of the shoes.

6 If a new wheel cylinder has been fitted, bleed the brakes (Section 15.3).

7 Adjust the brakes (Section 15.4).

15.8 Removing the brake master cylinder

The brake master cylinder is mounted inside a body member beneath the floor on the right-hand side of the driving compartment. Although topping-up the fluid level, as described in Section 15.1, presents no difficulties, the inaccessible position of the master cylinder does mean that it is often neglected for long periods and that leakage past the piston seals may go undetected.

It is advisable, therefore, to remove the inspection plate from the floor above the cylinder at least once a year — or say at 12 000 mile intervals — to give the cylinder a routine check.

A second snag is that the cylinder mounting bolts pass through the body member and although the nuts can be removed without difficulty, the torsion bar prevents the bolts being withdrawn.

The official instructions therefore say that the bar must be detached as described in Chapter 14, but as this entails a lot of work, including partially dismantling the front suspension, it is not surprising that practical owners try to avoid doing so if possible.

The usual method adopted in practice is to spring the bar down just sufficiently to allow the bolts to be withdrawn, using a well-padded lever and being careful not to nick the bar — which would create a stress point which might lead to fracture — and not to put a permanent bend in it.

Assuming that this method is adopted, the master cylinder can be removed and refitted as follows —

Materials: Any new parts required. Lockheed universal brake fluid. Penetrating oil or rust-releasing fluid.

Tools: Spanners. Lever for torsion bar. Jack. Axle stands.

1 Jack-up and support the car to give access to the underside of the floor.

2 Uncouple the brake pipe from the cylinder and seal the openings to prevent loss of fluid and the entry of dirt or grit. If the union is rusty, first soak it with penetrating oil or rust-releasing fluid and use a well-fitting spanner to avoid the risk of burring the edges of the hexagon.

3 Unscrew the nuts from the master cylinder mounting bolts, using two spanners. Carefully lever the bar down, clear of the heads of the bolts and extract them.

4 Remove the inspection plate from the floor above the master cylinder. Again, it would be wise to soak the retaining screws with penetrating oil or rust-releasing fluid in advance, as they can be reluctant to come out.

5 Uncouple the brake pipe from the banjo union at the back of the master cylinder.

6 The cylinder is now ready to be removed and although the official instructions say that it is necessary to withdraw the clutch and brake pedal cross-shaft and lift out the cylinder complete with the

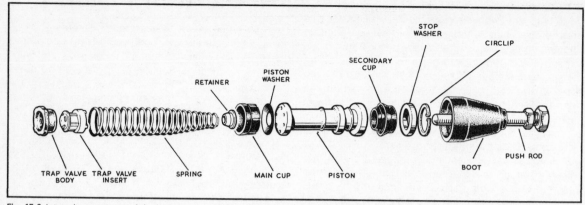

Fig. 15.6 Internal components of the brake master cylinder. This is a typical assembly, but minor differences may be found on early cars

brake-pedal assembly, in practice the cylinder can be fiddled out through the opening if the brake pedal is pressed down in order to give a better angle for extracting the cylinder.

7 Before refitting the cylinder, or a new cylinder, clean out the compartment and if necessary, paint it with a rust-preventing preparation. Also clean the end of the operating rod and smear it well with grease before fitting the new sealing boot. When installing the cylinder, the filler plug should be in place so that there is no risk of dirt or grit entering the filler hole.

8 The bolts *must* be refitted with their heads towards the bar. If they are inserted the other way round to make removal easier when the cylinder is next removed, the bar may contact the ends of the bolts when it flexes with the car heavily laden on a poor road surface, and may fracture.

9 Finally, when the pipes have been coupled-up, refill the cylinder with Lockheed universal brake fluid and then bleed the system as described in Section 15.3.

15.9 Servicing the brake hoses

During routine servicing the brake hoses should be inspected for signs of leakage, chafing or general

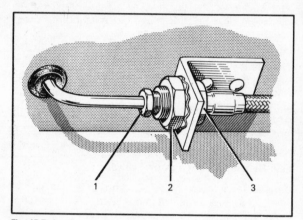

Fig. 15.7 A union coupling a rigid brake pipe to a flexible hose. The nut 1 must first be unscrewed, after which the nut 2 can be slackened, while holding the hose stationary with a spanner on the hexagon 3. When reassembling, tighten the parts in the reverse order

deterioration. They should in any case be renewed after 40 000 miles or every three years, whichever occurs first.

Scrupulous cleanliness is vital when removing and refitting the hoses.

16 The electrical system

No special electrical knowledge, or expensive test instruments, are needed for normal maintenance of the electrical equipment, nor should simple fault-tracing and first-aid measures present any problems. If any serious troubles crop-up, it is best to take advantage of the service-exchange scheme operated by your dealer, under which a faulty component is replaced by a reconditioned, guaranteed unit at a fixed charge (see also Chapter 8).

If an alternator is fitted instead of a dynamo, servicing and fault-tracing should be left to an auto-electrician.

When removing and replacing the battery, or when working on the system, remember that the positive battery terminal is earthed. As there will be both positive-earth and negative-earth systems in use for some years to come, special care must also be taken when ordering and installing replacement equipment and accessories such as a transistor-operated car radio, which will be seriously damaged if it is connected so that its polarity is reversed.

The time factor

The maintenance checks and simple servicing described in this chapter do not call for pre-planning, minor jobs taking only a few minutes each. Suggested times for more ambitious work are: removing and refitting the dynamo, 45 min; removing the starter motor, 30 min; overhauling a dynamo, 1½ hr, overhauling a starter motor, 2 hr.

16.1 Topping-up the battery cells

The liquid in the cells (the electrolyte) tends to evaporate rather quickly, especially in hot weather. Check the levels at weekly intervals and don't allow the electrolyte to fall below the tops of the separators between the plates, or the perforated separator guard, as the case may be.

Distilled or 'purified' water is obtainable quite cheaply from chemists. Tapwater and rainwater may contain impurities that will shorten the life of the battery. In an emergency, water from the drip-tray of a refrigerator which has been defrosted can be used, but *not* the water obtained by melting ice cubes.

Never use a naked flame when inspecting the fluid level. An explosive mixture of hydrogen and oxygen is produced when the electrolyte begins to bubble, as the battery becomes fully charged.

Add water just before the cells are to be charged, to allow the acid and water to mix thoroughly, and to avoid any risk of the water freezing, expanding and damaging the plates and battery case in cold weather.

The need for frequent topping-up usually suggests too high a generator charging rate. If one cell regularly requires more than the others, it is probably leaking. Unless the battery is nearly new, or still under guarantee, repairs to individual cells are not usually worthwhile.

It should not be necessary to add *acid* to the cells unless some of the electrolyte has been split, in which case it would be wise to have a word with your dealer.

Finally, remember that the electrolyte is a very corrosive solution of sulphuric acid in water. If any is spilled, wipe it away immediately with a clean wet cloth and then dry the part thoroughly. Household ammonia will neutralize the acid.

16.2 Battery maintenance

The tops of the cells must be kept clean and dry, to prevent corrosion of the terminals and leakage of current.

The battery-retaining clamp should be just sufficiently tight to prevent movement of the battery on its mounting. Overtightening it may crack or distort the battery case.

To clean the terminals and terminal posts —

1 Take off the connectors.

2 Scrape any corrosion off the terminals.

3 Replace the connectors and tighten the retaining screws. Smear the terminals and posts with petroleum jelly to protect them against corrosion.

4 Don't overlook the connections at the earthed end of the battery earthing strap, at the starter motor and at the starter switch. These connections must be clean and secure.

16.3 Ignition and dynamo warning light

A red warning light on the instrument panel glows whenever the generator is not producing an adequate supply of current. Although this lamp is usually termed the ignition warning light (because one of its functions is to remind you not to leave the ignition switched on when the engine is not running) it has the equally important function of warning that the generator is not charging. It should therefore be regarded as an *ignition and no-charge* warning light.

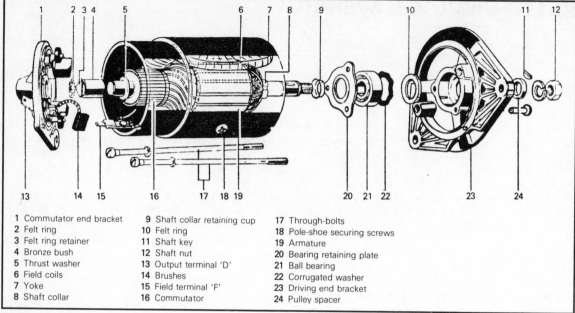

1 Commutator end bracket	9 Shaft collar retaining cup	17 Through-bolts
2 Felt ring	10 Felt ring	18 Pole-shoe securing screws
3 Felt ring retainer	11 Shaft key	19 Armature
4 Bronze bush	12 Shaft nut	20 Bearing retaining plate
5 Thrust washer	13 Output terminal 'D'	21 Ball bearing
6 Field coils	14 Brushes	22 Corrugated washer
7 Yoke	15 Field terminal 'F'	23 Driving end bracket
8 Shaft collar	16 Commutator	24 Pulley spacer

Fig. 16.1 The C40/1 type dynamo

If the light does not go out, or glows faintly when the engine is speeded up above idling speed, the battery is not receiving a charge and will quickly become discharged if the trouble is not put right without delay. First check that the fan belt is intact and correctly tensioned (Chapter 10). Then have the generator and regulator checked by an electrical specialist, or make the tests described in Section 16.15.

16.4 Servicing a dynamo

1 Check and if necessary adjust the tension of the driving belt as described in Chapter 10, and lubricate the rear bearing by applying a few drops of engine oil to the bearing housing at the opposite end of the dynamo to the pulley at 6000-mile (10 000 km) intervals.

2 Specialist attention (say at 36 000-mile, 60 000 km, intervals) includes inspection and cleaning of the commutator and brushes. It is preferable to leave this to your dealer, who will also be able to check and adjust the charging regulator, but if necessary the dynamo can be serviced at home as follows (Section 16.5).

16.5 Inspecting and cleaning the dynamo commutator and brushes

If the commutator and brushes require servicing, it is necessary to remove the dynamo and to take off the end-plate at the opposite end to the driving pulley.

Materials: New brushes. Paraffin or petrol.
Tools: Screwdriver. Pliers.

1 Remove the dynamo and take out the long bolts that retain the end-plate. With the plate removed the driving end bracket and the armature can be withdrawn. The commutator, an assembly of copper segments at the end of the rotating armature, and the brushes, can then be examined.

2 Clean the commutator. If it is scored, take it to an electrical specialist, who will skim it in a lathe.

3 Check that the brushes move freely in their holders. If they stick, clean them and their holders with a cloth moistened with petrol. If the brushes have worn down to a minimum length of about $\frac{1}{4}$ in. (6 mm), renew them. If worn but serviceable brushes are refitted, make sure that they are inserted in their original positions, to maintain the correct 'bedding'.

4 When reassembling the end-plate that carries the brushes trap the brushes in the raised position in their holders, clear of the commutator, by side pressure from their springs, and finally position the springs correctly by passing a screwdriver through the inspection holes in the plate when the latter is fully home.

16.6 Starter motor servicing

The starter motor is probably the most important of the auxiliaries that draw current from the battery. Unlike the generator, it is in action only intermittently and usually has a long, trouble-free life. Because it requires no periodic lubrication it is, in fact, often overlooked by the average owner.

The starter should be serviced at reasonable intervals — say, every 36 000 miles (60 000 km) — when it should be removed from the car and dismantled so that the commutator, brushes and the

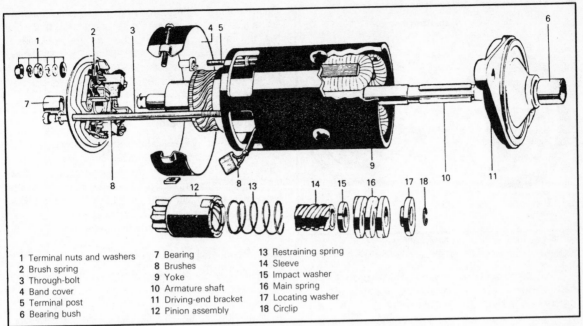

1 Terminal nuts and washers	7 Bearing	13 Restraining spring
2 Brush spring	8 Brushes	14 Sleeve
3 Through-bolt	9 Yoke	15 Impact washer
4 Band cover	10 Armature shaft	16 Main spring
5 Terminal post	11 Driving-end bracket	17 Locating washer
6 Bearing bush	12 Pinion assembly	18 Circlip

Fig. 16.2 An exploded view of the starter motor and drive

pinion-drive components can be inspected and cleaned.

To overhaul the starter —

Materials: New brushes and drive parts, as needed. Paraffin or CTC. Clean cloth.

Tools: Screwdriver. Pliers. Drive spring compressing tool.

1 Remove the inspection cover band.

2 Hold back the brush springs and extract the brushes.

3 Unscrew the through-bolts and take off the commutator-end bracket, and the driving-end bracket complete with the armature and drive assembly.

4 Clean the commutator and if it is badly scored, have it reconditioned by an auto-electrician.

5 To fit new brushes, the old leads must be unsoldered and the new leads soldered to the terminal eyes and the tappings on the field coils.

6 To dismantle the drive components, either remove the split-pin and retaining nut if fitted, or compress the spring and remove the circlip from the end of the shaft. A spring compressor can be bought from an accessory shop. When reassembling the drive do not lubricate the parts.

The headlamps

The headlamps are fitted either with sealed-beam light units or with separate reflectors and lamp bulbs. Sealed-beam units form, in effect, large bulbs, each with either one or two filaments, an integral reflector and a front lens. Consequently, when a filament burns out, it is necessary to renew the complete unit. For some export markets, however, conventional reflector and front lens assemblies may be fitted, and in this case the separate bulbs can be renewed.

16.7 Adjusting the headlamp beam

It is particularly important that the headlamp beams should be correctly aligned. Hit-and-miss methods of adjustment in the home garage are likely to result in settings that dazzle oncoming traffic or do not give the most effective illumination.

Fig. 16.3 The screws indicated by the arrows retain the headlamp reflector and are also used to adjust its position while aligning the beam

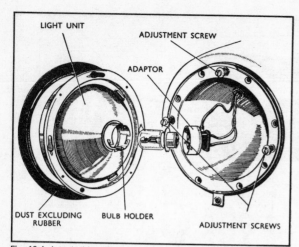

LIGHT UNIT

ADJUSTMENT SCREW

ADAPTOR

DUST EXCLUDING RUBBER

BULB HOLDER

ADJUSTMENT SCREWS

Fig. 16.4 A typical headlamp assembly, with the light unit — the reflector and front lens — removed to give access to the bulb

Most garages today, however, have optical beam-setting equipment which enables the lamps to be precisely adjusted. The headlamp settings should be checked with the aid of such equipment twice a year if a lot of night driving is done, or at least once every autumn.

1 Remove the lamp rim, which is retained by a screw at the base.

2 Rotate the upper adjusting screw (Fig. 16.4) to adjust the lamp vertically, and the screw at one or both sides to swing the beam horizontally. Make allowances for the fact that the beam will be raised when passengers and luggage are carried in the rear of the car.

16.8 Renewing the headlamp bulbs or sealed-beam units

1 It is unnecessary to disturb the setting of the adjusting screws when removing the combined reflector and lamp glass units, unless the screws have been tightened to such an extent that it is impossible to rotate the reflector anti-clockwise when it has been pushed back against the resistance of the three springs, in order to allow the openings in the slots to register with the heads of the screws. In such a case the adjusting screws should be slackened-off and the headlamp should be realigned when the light unit has been replaced — see Section 16.7. The way in which the bulb is retained by a bayonet cap is clearly shown in Fig. 16.4.

2 The headlamps fitted to later models may have sealed-beam units in which the filaments are enclosed within combined, glass lens-reflector assemblies. If a lamp filament should fail, therefore, it will be necessary to replace the complete unit. Fortunately these have a very much longer life than ordinary lamp bulbs and the reflectors, of course, cannot become dulled or tarnished. To renew a unit, take off the headlamp rim

dust excluder, after removing the retaining screw, slacken the three screws that secure the rim that holds the unit in place and rotate the rim anti-clockwise to disengage it from the screw heads. Do not slacken the screws that allow the lamp beam to be aimed, one at the top of the lamp and one on one side or both sides of the reflector.

16.9 Side and rear lamps

When the lamp glass is retained by a screw or a pair of screws, the method of removing it is self-evident. In other cases the glass and its plated rim are retained by a flange in the moulded rubber surround and can be renewed without difficulty by folding back the rubber with the fingers. Always replace the glass first, followed by the rim — not the two together.

16.10 Panel and warning lamps

In order to renew the panel or warning lamp bulbs the instrument dial must be drawn forward into the car. The assembly is retained by a captive cross-head screw at each side. A small hole is provided in the inner wall of each glove compartment through which it is possible to insert a screwdriver of the cross-head type, to engage with the screw.

16.11 The windscreen wiper

The electrically-operated windscreen wiper normally requires no attention, other than renewal of the wiper blades at least once a year. Even blades that are in good condition cannot be effective, however, if the glass has acquired a coating of 'traffic film', consisting largely of deposits caused by exhaust fumes (diesel-engined vehicles are particularly bad offenders in this respect) which result in persistent smearing of the raindrops in the path of the wiper blades. The silicones used in many modern car polishes can create a similar effect.

In either case the most satisfactory remedy is to clean the screen and blades with a windscreen-washer detergent, used undiluted. In no circumstances use abrasives as the glass is easily scratched. For the same reason, the wiper blades should not be kept in action on a dry screen.

If the blades do not sweep through satisfactory arcs, or fail to park neatly, it is possible that at some time the arms have been incorrectly fitted to the driving spindles. The arms engage with fine splines cut on the spindles, so that very accurate positioning is possible. Each arm is retained by a small spring clip, positioned just beneath the pivot pin, which must be lifted out of engagement with the slot in the spindle with the aid of a small screwdriver or similar tool, before the arm can be drawn off.

It is not always realized that the windscreen-wiper motor embodies an adjustable switch that controls the parking position of the arms. To reset the switch,

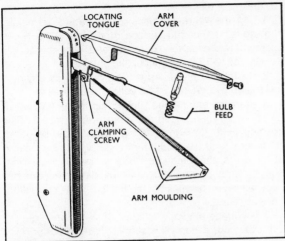

LOCATING TONGUE
ARM COVER
ARM CLAMPING SCREW
BULB FEED
ARM MOULDING

Fig. 16.5 An earlier, semaphore-type, direction indicator

remove both arms from their spindles, slacken the three cover securing screws on the wiper motor and rotate the automatic parking switch until the two rivet heads are positioned at 'one o'clock' to the drive cable, pointing towards the cable outlet. The cover screws should then be tightened and the motor switched on and off in order to operate the parking switch. The wiper arms should then be refitted to the spindle with each arm in the parked position. Before checking the effect of this adjustment, wet the screen in order to prevent excessive drag on the wiper blades.

16.12 Semaphore direction indicators

The semaphore-type trafficators fitted to earlier cars seldom require attention other than lubrication of the pivot pin at 6000-mile intervals. Sooner or later, however, a bulb will require renewal and the possibility of an arm being damaged or fractured while in the extended position cannot be entirely ruled out.

When an indicator fails to rise or does not return fully into its socket the most usual cause is bending or distortion of the arm, caused by accidental damage. It is often possible to straighten the arm by applying gentle pressure with the fingers, taking care not to place any strain on the pivot or actuating mechanism. If the translucent moulding has been cracked or fractured it can be renewed by taking off the top cover as described below and slackening the clamping screw that retains the moulding in the metal section of the arm. If a new moulding is not immediately available, it is usually possible to effect a temporary repair with one of the modern adhesives that are specifically intended for use on plastics. Ordinary liquid glues are seldom effective for any appreciable period.

To change a bulb —

1 Raise the arm by switching it on and supporting it while the switch is returned to the 'off' position. Any attempt to lever the arm out of its housing with a screwdriver is liable to damage the locking mechanism.

2 Remove the top cover by unscrewing the securing screw at the upper end. Before fitting the new bulb, make sure that the contact spring is not corroded or flattened, and brighten the point on the underside of the top cover at which the bulb will make contact.

16.13 Flashing indicators

When flashing indicators are fitted instead of the semaphore type, the indicator lamps are fed with intermittent current from a sealed control unit. This contains a switch which is actuated by the alternate expansion and contraction of a length of wire that is heated by the current passing to the indicator lamps, thus giving a flashing frequency of about 60-120 times per minute.

On some earlier models the rear indicator lamps function also as stop lamps and in these cases a relay is interposed in the circuit which overrides the action of the brake switch, ensuring that response to the flasher unit takes precedence over simultaneous depression of the brake pedal.

Failure or erratic action of the flashing indicators may be caused by dirty contacts in the indicator switch or in the relay, or by a faulty flasher unit. While the former units can be serviced by anyone with a little electrical knowledge, the flasher unit is not repairable. A replacement unit should be handled with care as it is a somewhat delicate component and can be put out of action if it is dropped or receives a moderately hard knock.

16.14 Testing and renewing a faulty brake stop-light switch

The stop-lamp switch, which is operated by the hydraulic pressure in the braking system, is incorporated in the T-union at the point at which the pipeline from the master cylinder joins the pipe that feeds the front brakes.

1 If the stop-lights flicker or fail to come on when the brake pedal is depressed and the lamp bulbs, holders and wiring have been checked and found to be in order, disconnect the two wires from the pressure switch and, with the ignition switched on, touch them together. If the stop-lamps then light up either the switch is faulty or the leads were making poor contact with the terminals. A faulty switch should be replaced by a new one and the front brakes should then be bled.

2 If the stop-lights do not come on when the switch leads are short-circuited, a fault must obviously exist at some point in the wiring, either between the A4 terminal on the fuse unit and the switch, or between the switch and the stop-and-tail lamp holders.

16.15 The fuses

Two fuses are carried in clips on a holder attached to the engine bulkhead, which also houses two spares.

The 50-amp fuse fitted between the clips marked A1 and A2 protects the accessories which can be operated whether or not the ignition is switched on — for example the interior light and the horn.

The fuse between the clips marked A3 and A4 is of 35-amp rating and protects those items, such as the stop lamp, fuel gauge, oil-pressure warning light, trafficators, and windscreen wipers, which operate only when the ignition is switched on.

On later models there is a third fuse, rated at 10 amp, in a bayonet-type holder inserted in a, wire beneath the regulator and fuse box. This protects the side and rear lights.

A fuse must always be replaced by one which has the same rating as the original. The headlamp circuits, incidentally, are not protected by a fuse.

Failure of a particular fuse is indicated when the circuit protected by it becomes 'dead'. If a new fuse burns out immediately, find the cause and rectify the fault before fitting a new fuse having the same rating, which is shown on a coloured slip of paper inside the fuse. *Never be tempted to bridge the fuse-holder clips with ordinary wire,* as this can lead to a fire in the wiring, or a burnt-out component.

Simple fault-tracing

A thorough diagnosis of an ailing electrical system calls for the use of proper fault-tracing equipment, or at least an accurate moving-coil voltmeter. Ideally, a special instrument tester should be used to check the fuel and temperature gauges, so this sort of work is outside the scope of the average owner.

There are, however, some simple tests that can be made when it is suspected that the dynamo is not giving its full charge, or when the starter motor does not turn the engine.

16.16 Testing the dynamo and charging system

The following tests, for which only a voltmeter is required, are sufficient to show whether or not all is well with the dynamo and the charging system. A moving-coil type of meter is to be preferred, but any good-quality instrument can be used, as the checks depend on comparative readings, rather than on exact voltages. They are based on the fact that the battery voltage varies according to the state of charge, and is always higher when the cells are receiving a charge from the dynamo.

To make the test —

1 Clip the voltmeter leads to the battery terminals, making sure that the surface of the metal has been pierced. If the battery is sound and well charged, a reading of 12-12.5 volts should be obtained.

2 Switch on all the lights. The reading should now fall to approximately 11-11.5 volts.

3 Start the engine and speed it up to the equivalent of about 20 mph in top gear, but do not race it. The reading (with the lights still on) should now be about 13.5 volts, and the voltmeter needle should be steady. If it flickers, there may be a bad contact in the wiring, the dynamo commutator may be dirty, the brushes may be worn or sticking, or the cut-out or regulator may be faulty.

4 If voltage readings roughly equal to those quoted are obtained, it can be assumed that the battery and charging system are sound. If the voltage across the battery does not rise by 1 volt when the engine is speeded-up above idling speed, there is a fault somewhere in the charging system, probably one of those just mentioned. If the increase exceeds about 1.5 volts, either the regulator is incorrectly adjusted or the battery is faulty. Do not try to adjust the regulator. Leave this sort of work to a qualified auto-electrician.

16.17 Testing a faulty starter motor

1 Switch on the lights and press the starter switch. If the solenoid switch clicks and the lights go dim, but the starter does not operate, either the battery is discharged or current is flowing through the windings of the starter but for some reason the armature is not rotating. Probably the starter pinion is jammed in mesh with the flywheel starter ring.

2 The easiest way to free a jammed starter pinion is to switch off the ignition, engage *top gear* and rock the car *forwards*. Do not rock the car backwards and forwards, as this may jam the pinion more firmly in mesh with the flywheel ring-gear teeth. If this does not work it will be necessary to turn the squared end of the starter motor spindle (beneath the ignition distributor) in a clockwise direction with a spanner to disengage the pinion. If a cap is fitted over the end of the spindle, prise it off and refit it afterwards.

3 If the lamps remain bright, the starter switch may be faulty, but first check for loose or corroded connections on the ignition switch or on the electro-magnetic solenoid starter switch itself, which is mounted on the engine bulkhead.

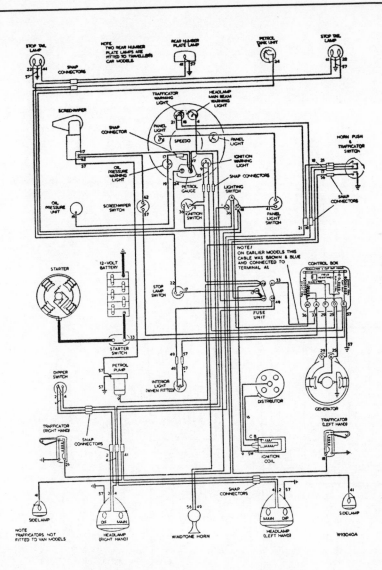

Key to cable colours

	16 White with black	34 Brown with red	52 Purple with blue
	17 Green	35 Brown with yellow	53 Purple with white
	18 Green with red	36 Brown with blue	54 Purple with green
1 Blue	19 Green with yellow	37 Brown with white	55 Purple with brown
2 Blue with red	20 Green with blue	38 Brown with green	56 Purple with black
3 Blue with yellow	21 Green with white	39 Brown with purple	57 Black
4 Blue with white	22 Green with purple	40 Brown with black	58 Black with red
5 Blue with green	23 Green with brown	41 Red	59 Black with yellow
6 Blue with purple	24 Green with black	42 Red with yellow	60 Black with blue
7 Blue with brown	25 Yellow	43 Red with blue	61 Black with white
8 Blue with black	26 Yellow with red	44 Red with white	62 Black with green
9 White	27 Yellow with blue	45 Red with green	63 Black with purple
10 White with red	28 Yellow with white	46 Red with purple	64 Black with brown
11 White with yellow	29 Yellow with green	47 Red with brown	65 Dark green
12 White with blue	30 Yellow with purple	48 Red with black	66 Light green
13 White with green	31 Yellow with brown	49 Purple	
14 White with purple	32 Yellow with black	50 Purple with red	
15 White with brown	33 Brown	51 Purple with yellow	

Fig. 16.6 Wiring diagram for the 1956-7 models

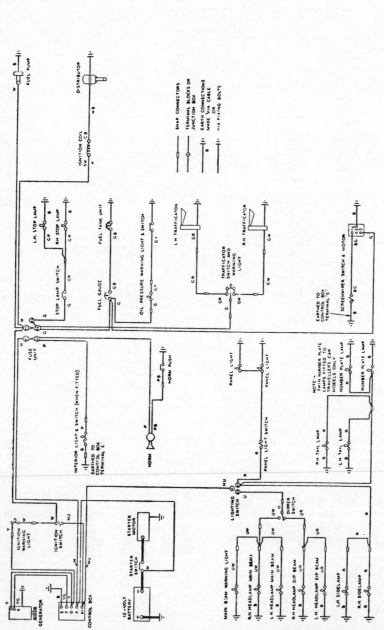

When a cable has two colour code letters, the first denotes the main colour and the second denotes the tracer colour

Fig. 16.7 Wiring diagram for the 1958-60 models

Key to cable colours

B Black
U Blue
N Brown
R Red
P Purple
G Green
S Slate
W White
Y Yellow
D Dark
L Light
M Medium

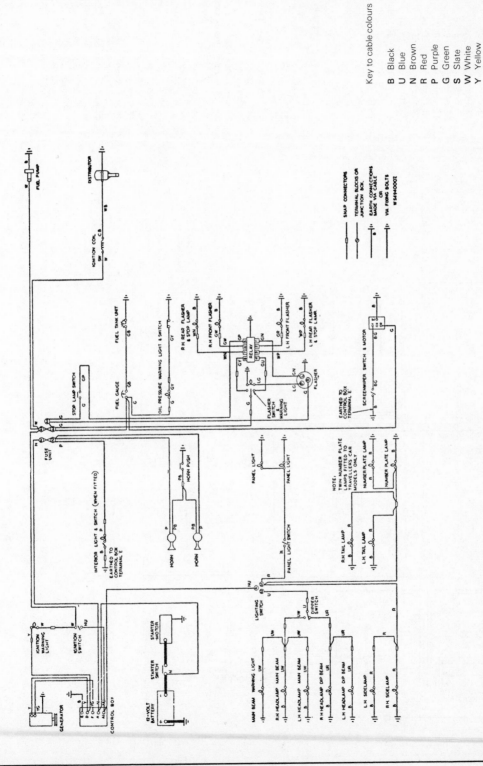

Fig. 16.8 Wiring diagram for cars with flashing indicators

When a cable has two colour code letters, the first denotes the main colour and the second the tracer colour

Key to cable colours

B Black
U Blue
N Brown
R Red
P Purple
G Green
S Slate
W White
Y Yellow
D Dark
L Light
M Medium

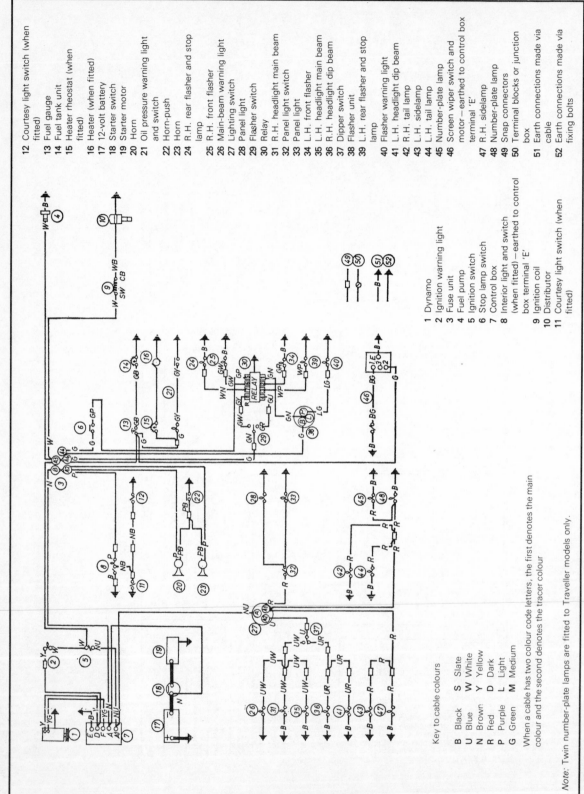

12 Courtesy light switch (when fitted)
13 Fuel gauge
14 Fuel tank unit
15 Heater rheostat (when fitted)
16 Heater (when fitted)
17 12-volt battery
18 Starter switch
19 Starter motor
20 Horn
21 Oil pressure warning light and switch
22 Horn-push
23 Horn
24 R.H. rear flasher and stop lamp
25 R.H. front flasher
26 Main-beam warning light
27 Lighting switch
28 Panel light
29 Flasher switch
30 Relay
31 R.H. headlight main beam
32 Panel light switch
33 Panel light
34 L.H. front flasher
35 L.H. headlight main beam
36 R.H. headlight dip beam
37 Dipper switch
38 Flasher unit
39 L.H. rear flasher and stop lamp
40 Flasher warning light
41 L.H. headlight dip beam
42 R.H. tail lamp
43 L.H. sidelamp
44 L.H. tail lamp
45 Number-plate lamp
46 Screen wiper switch and motor – earthed to control box terminal 'E'
47 R.H. sidelamp
48 Number-plate lamp
49 Snap connectors
50 Terminal blocks or junction box
51 Earth connections made via cable
52 Earth connections made via fixing bolts

1 Dynamo
2 Ignition warning light
3 Fuse unit
4 Fuel pump
5 Ignition switch
6 Stop lamp switch
7 Control box
8 Interior light and switch (when fitted) – earthed to control box terminal 'E'
9 Ignition coil
10 Distributor
11 Courtesy light switch (when fitted)

Key to cable colours

B	Black	S	Slate
U	Blue	W	White
N	Brown	Y	Yellow
R	Red	D	Dark
P	Purple	L	Light
G	Green	M	Medium

When a cable has two colour code letters, the first denotes the main colour and the second denotes the tracer colour

Note: Twin number-plate lamps are fitted to Traveller models only.

Fig. 16.9 Wiring diagram for cars fitted with courtesy-light door switches

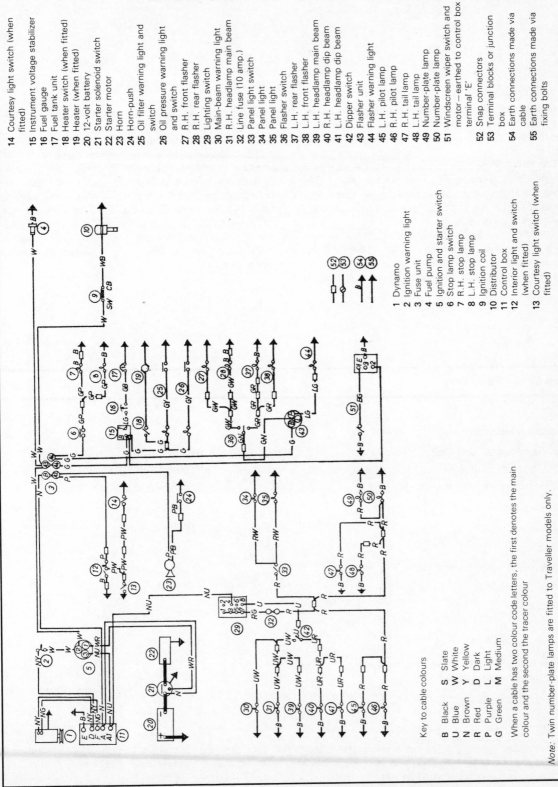

14 Courtesy light switch (when fitted)
15 Instrument voltage stabilizer
16 Fuel gauge
17 Fuel tank unit
18 Heater switch (when fitted)
19 Heater (when fitted)
20 12-volt battery
21 Starter solenoid switch
22 Starter motor
23 Horn
24 Horn-push
25 Oil filter warning light and switch
26 Oil pressure warning light and switch
27 R.H. front flasher
28 R.H. rear flasher
29 Lighting switch
30 Main-beam warning light
31 R.H. headlamp main beam
32 Line fuse (10 amp.)
33 Panel light switch
34 Panel light
35 Panel light
36 Flasher switch
37 L.H. rear flasher
38 L.H. front flasher
39 L.H. headlamp main beam
40 R.H. headlamp dip beam
41 L.H. headlamp dip beam
42 Dipper switch
43 Flasher unit
44 Flasher warning light
45 L.H. pilot lamp
46 R.H. pilot lamp
47 R.H. tail lamp
48 L.H. tail lamp
49 Number-plate lamp
50 Number-plate lamp
51 Windscreen wiper switch and motor—earthed to control box terminal 'E'
52 Snap connectors
53 Terminal blocks or junction box
54 Earth connections made via cable
55 Earth connections made via fixing bolts

1 Dynamo
2 Ignition warning light
3 Fuse unit
4 Fuel pump
5 Ignition and starter switch
6 Stop lamp switch
7 R.H. stop lamp
8 L.H. stop lamp
9 Ignition coil
10 Distributor
11 Control box
12 Interior light and switch (when fitted)
13 Courtesy light switch (when fitted)

Key to cable colours

B Black   S Slate
U Blue   W White
N Brown   Y Yellow
R Red   D Dark
P Purple   L Light
G Green   M Medium

When a cable has two colour code letters, the first denotes the main colour and the second the tracer colour.

Note: Twin number-plate lamps are fitted to Traveller models only.

Fig. 16.10 Wiring diagram for later models with the starter motor controlled by the ignition switch.

17 Specifications and overhaul data

In this chapter we have included the specifications and data which will be needed to carry out the adjustments and overhauls which are likely to be within the scope of a d.i.y. owner.

We have avoided giving lists of fits, clearances and engineering tolerances which call for the use of micrometers and similar precision equipment, however, as these are not likely to be found — or needed — in the average home garage.

As we recommend in Chapter 8, highly-skilled work of this sort should be left to a Leyland dealer or to a specialist who is best qualified to handle it. Alternatively it is often possible to fit reconditioned components, the cost of which can show a considerable saving over the price of new parts.

Some of the more important nuts and bolts must be tightened to a specified torque figure, expressed in lb ft and Nm, to ensure the correct tightness without the risk of overstressing a bolt or nut or distorting a part. The tightening torques for the more critical components have therefore been included in the data tables.

When self-locking nuts are fitted, these should not be re-used if their self-locking effect has been reduced. They should not be degreased. As a precaution, it is better to fit new nuts.

Top-up and fill-up data

Capacities (approx.)

Petrol tank: up to April 1957	5 gal (22.7 litres)
April 1957 on	6½ gal (29.6 litres)
Engine oil sump (with filter change)	6½ – 7 pints (3.7 – 3.98 litres)
Oil filter capacity	1 pint (0.57 litre)
Gearbox	2¼ pints (1.3 litres)
Rear axle	1½ pints (0.85 litre)
Cooling system (including heater)	9¾ pints (5.57 litres)
Heater capacity	1 pint (0.57 litre)

Recommended fuel grades

3-star petrol (94 octane minimum) may be usable but if the engine pinks or runs-on after switching off, use 4-star (97 octane minimum).

Oil consumption

A reasonable consumption for a worn engine is about 500 miles per pint. The figure for a new or reconditioned engine may be as high as 350 miles per pint, gradually improving during the first 2000 – 3000 miles as the piston rings and cylinder walls bed-in.

Recommended lubricants — temperate climates

Engine	Multigrade oil 10W/40, 10W/50, 15W/50, 20W/40, 20W/50
Ignition distributor shaft, contact-breaker pivot, automatic timing control, dynamo bearing	Engine oil
Carburettor damper	20W/50 engine oil
Gearbox	Engine oil
Rear axle	Hypoid gear oil 90EP
Front-wheel hub bearings	Multipurpose lithium grease
Grease-gun points	Multipurpose lithium grease

Engine — see Chapter 9

All models are water-cooled, four-cylinder, in-line engines with push-rod-operated overhead valves.

	1956-1962 models	Models from October 1962 on
Capacity	948 cc (57.85 cu in.)	1098 cc (67 cu in.)
Cylinder bore	62.93 mm (2.478 in.)	64.58 mm (2.543 in.)
Piston stroke	76.2 mm (3.00 in.)	83.72 mm (3.296 in.)
Compression ratio	8.3 : 1	8.5 : 1 (7.5 : 1 alternative on van)
Maximum brake-horsepower (net)	37 bhp at 4750 rpm	48 bhp at 5100 rpm (43 bhp with lower compression ratio)

Engine lubrication, maintenance and repair

Oil grade	See recommended lubricants on this page
Oil filter	Replaceable element
Oil pressure: normal running	60 lb/sq in. (4.2 kg/cm² or bars)
idling	15 lb/sq in. (1.05 kg/cm² or bars)
Valve clearance: cold	0.012 in. (0.30 mm)
hot	0.011 in. (0.28 mm)
Piston clearance in cylinder bore —	
948 cc: Top of skirt	0.0021 − 0.0039 in. (0.053 − 0.099 mm)
Bottom of skirt	0.0006 − 0.0024 in. (0.015 − 0.061 mm)
1098 cc: Top of skirt	0.0021 − 0.0037 in. (0.053 − 0.094 mm)
Bottom of skirt	0.0005 − 0.0011 in. (0.013 − 0.28 mm)
Gudgeon pin fit: 948 cc	Clamped in little end, floating fit in piston
1098 cc	Fully floating, hand push-fit in piston at room temperature

Connecting-rod big-end diametrical clearance:

948 cc	0.0006 – 0.0016 in. (0.015 – 0.041 mm)
1098 cc	0.001 – 0.0025 in. (0.025 – 0.064 mm)

Connecting-rod big-end side clearance: 948 cc   0.008 – 0.010 in. (0.203 – 0.254 mm)
1098 cc   0.008 – 0.012 in. (0.203 – 0.305 mm)

Main bearing diametrical clearance: 948 cc   0.001 – 0.002 in. (0.025 – 0.051 mm)
1098 cc   0.001 – 0.0027 in. (0.025 – 0.068 mm)

Crankshaft end-float   0.002 – 0.003 in. (0.051 – 0.076 mm)

Camshaft bearing clearance   0.001 – 0.002 in. (0.025 – 0.051 mm)

Camshaft end-float   0.003 – 0.007 in. (0.076 – 0.178 mm)

Valve clearance in guide: inlet, 948 cc, 1098 cc   0.0015 – 0.0025 in. (0.038 – 0.064 mm)
exhaust, 948 cc   0.0010 – 0.0019 in. (0.025 – 0.048 mm)
1098 cc   0.002 – 0.003 in. (0.051 – 0.076 mm)

Torque-wrench settings

	lb ft	Nm
Cylinder-head stud nuts	40	54
Connecting-rod big-end bolts, 948 cc	33	45
1098 cc	35	47
Main bearing stud nuts, 948 cc	65	88
Main bearing set screws, 1098 cc	60	81
Flywheel attachment bolts, 948 cc	50	68
1098 cc	35 – 40	47 – 54
Rocker-shaft bracket nuts	25	34
Water pump	17	23
Water outlet elbow	8	11
Oil filter bolt	16	22
Oil pump	9	12
Manifold to cylinder head	15	20
Crankshaft pulley nut	70	95

Cooling system – see Chapter 10

Type   Thermostatically controlled, pressurized
system with engine-driven pump and fan

Expansion tank filler-cap pressure   4 lb/sq in. (0.28 kg/cm² or bars)

Thermostat   Bellows type
Opening temperature: without heater   72°C (162°F)
with heater   80 – 85°C (176 – 185°F)

Carburettor and petrol pump — see Chapter 11

Carburettor: up to 1960	SU H2
1960 on	SU HS2
Carburettor needle — standard	
SU H2 carburettor with oil-bath air cleaner (early models)	BX1
SU H2 carburettor with paper-element air cleaner (later models)	M
SU HS2 carburettor: 948 cc models	M
1098 cc models	AN
Piston ring colour code	Red
Petrol pump	SU electric

Ignition system — see Chapter 12

Firing order	1, 3, 4, 2 (No. 1 cylinder is next to the radiator)
Sparking plugs	Champion N5 or equivalent type and grade
Sparking-plug gap	0.025 in. (0.64 mm)
Distributor	Lucas DM2A4
Contact-breaker gap	0.014 — 0.016 in. (0.36 — 0.40 mm)
Ignition timing	
948 cc: APJM/L engine	4° btdc
APJM/H engine	5° btdc
APJM/H engine (alternative: for cars using fuel of an octane value not exceeding 83)	tdc
1098 cc engine	3° btdc

Clutch and gearbox — see Chapter 13

Clutch type	Borg and Beck single dry plate, coil-spring type, mechanically operated
Free movement at clutch pedal	$\frac{3}{4}$ in. (19 mm) approx.
Gearbox	Synchromesh on second, third and fourth gears

Suspension, steering, tyres — see Chapter 14

Steering gear	Rack-and-pinion
Steering-wheel turns, lock-to-lock	2.6
Front-wheel toe-in	$\frac{3}{32}$ in. (2.5mm)

Checks on the steering geometry — castor, camber and steering pivot inclination angles and front-wheel alignment — call for the use of special equipment and this work must therefore be carried out by a Leyland dealer.

Tyres

The pressures given below are average figures only. The latest recommendations by the manufacturers of the tyres fitted to your car should always be checked, as there are sometimes variations between different makes of tyre. Most garages and tyre specialists should have this information.

Tyre size: earlier models	5.00 — 14
later models and 6 cwt van	5.20 — 14
8 cwt van	5.60 — 14

Tyre pressures

Saloon: normally laden, front and rear	22 lb/sq in. (1.55 kg/cm² or bars)
fully laden, front	22 lb/sq in. (1.55 kg/cm² or bars)
fully laden, rear	24 lb/sq in. (1.7 kg/cm² or bars)
Traveller: front	22 lb/sq in. (1.55 kg/cm² or bars)
rear	24 lb/sq in. (1.7 kg/cm² or bars)
Van: front	22 lb/sq in. (1.55 kg/cm² or bars)
rear (6 cwt)	27 lb/sq in. (1.89 kg/cm² or bars)
rear (8 cwt)	30 lb/sq in. (2.11 kg/cm² or bars)

(*Note:* Originally GPO vans had correct tyre pressures marked on vehicle sides)

Torque-wrench setting: Front hub nut	35 — 40 lb ft (47 — 54 Nm)

Braking system — see Chapter 15

Brake type	Lockheed hydraulic drum brakes at front and rear
Brake fluid	Lockheed Universal or Unipart

Electrical system — see Chapter 16

12-volt. Positive terminal of battery earthed. Dynamo with compensated voltage control regulator or Lucas 11 AC alternator.

Weights and measures — approx.

Overall length: Saloon	12 ft 4 in. (3.76 m)
Traveller	12 ft 5in. (3.785 m)
Van	11 ft 10$\frac{3}{8}$ in. (3.616m)
Overall width	5 ft 1 in. (1.55 m)
Overall height: Saloon	5 ft 0 in. (1.52 m)
Traveller	5 ft 0$\frac{1}{2}$ in. (1.54m)
Van	5ft 5$\frac{3}{4}$ in. (1.67 m)
Ground clearance	6$\frac{3}{4}$ in. (171 mm)
Turning circle	33 ft (10 m)
Weight: Two-door and Tourer	15 cwt (762 kg)
Four-door	15$\frac{1}{2}$ cwt (787 kg)
Traveller	16$\frac{1}{4}$ cwt (826 kg)
Van	15$\frac{1}{3}$ cwt (779 kg)

For maximum stability and safety when towing, it is recommended that the loaded weight of a caravan or trailer should not exceed three-quarters of the kerbside weight of the car.

Metric conversion tables

Inches	Decimals	Milli-metres	Inches to millimetres		Millimetres to inches		Fahrenheit & Centigrade			
			in.	mm	mm	in.	°F	°C	°C	°F
1/64	0·015625	0·3969	0·0001	0·00254	0·001	0·000039	−20	−28·9	−30	−22
1/32	0·03125	0·7937	0·0002	0·00508	0·002	0·000079	−15	−26·1	−28	−18·4
3/64	0·046875	1·1906	0·0003	0·00762	0·003	0·000118	−10	−23·3	−26	−14·8
1/16	0·0625	1·5875	0·0004	0·01016	0·004	0·000157	−5	−20·6	−24	−11·2
5/64	0·078125	1·9844	0·0005	0·01270	0·005	0·000197	0	−17·8	−22	−7·6
3/32	0·09375	2·3812	0·0006	0·01524	0·006	0·000236	1	−17·2	−20	−4
7/64	0·109375	2·7781	0·0007	0·01778	0·007	0·000276	2	−16·7	−18	−0·4
1/8	0·125	3·1750	0·0008	0·02032	0·008	0·000315	3	−16·1	−16	3·2
9/64	0·140625	3·5719	0·0009	0·02286	0·009	0·000354	4	−15·6	−14	6·8
5/32	0·15625	3·9687	0·001	0·0254	0·01	0·00039	5	−15·0	−12	10·4
11/64	0·171875	4·3656	0·002	0·0508	0·02	0·00079	10	−12·2	−10	14
3/16	0·1875	4·7625	0·003	0·0762	0·03	0·00118	15	−9·4	−8	17·6
13/64	0·203125	5·1594	0·004	0·1016	0·04	0·00157	20	−6·7	−6	21·2
7/32	0·21875	5·5562	0·005	0·1270	0·05	0·00197	25	−3·9	−4	24·8
15/64	0·234375	5·9531	0·006	0·1524	0·06	0·00236	30	−1·1	−2	28·4
1/4	0·25	6·3500	0·007	0·1778	0·07	0·00276	35	1·7	0	32
17/64	0·265625	6·7469	0·008	0·2032	0·08	0·00315	40	4·4	2	35·6
9/32	0·28125	7·1437	0·009	0·2286	0·09	0·00354	45	7·2	4	39·2
19/64	0·296875	7·5406	0·01	0·254	0·1	0·00394	50	10·0	6	42·8
5/16	0·3125	7·9375	0·02	0·508	0·2	0·00787	55	12·8	8	46·4
21/64	0·328125	8·3344	0·03	0·762	0·3	0·01181	60	15·6	10	50
11/32	0·34375	8·7312	0·04	1·016	0·4	0·01575	65	18·3	12	53·6
23/64	0·359375	9·1281	0·05	1·270	0·5	0·01969	70	21·1	14	57·2
3/8	0·375	9·5250	0·06	1·524	0·6	0·02362	75	23·9	16	60·8
25/64	0·390625	9·9219	0·07	1·778	0·7	0·02756	80	26·7	18	64·4
13/32	0·40625	10·3187	0·08	2·032	0·8	0·03150	85	29·4	20	68
27/64	0·421875	10·7156	0·09	2·286	0·9	0·03543	90	32·2	22	71·6
7/16	0·4375	11·1125	0·1	2·54	1	0·03937	95	35·0	24	75·2
29/64	0·453125	11·5094	0·2	5·08	2	0·07874	100	37·8	26	78·8
15/32	0·46875	11·9062	0·3	7·62	3	0·11811	105	40·6	28	82·4
31/64	0·484375	12·3031	0·4	10·16	4	0·15748	110	43·3	30	86
1/2	0·5	12·7000	0·5	12·70	5	0·19685	115	46·1	32	89·6
33/64	0·515625	13·0969	0·6	15·24	6	0·23622	120	48·9	34	93·2
17/32	0·53125	13·4937	0·7	17·78	7	0·27559	125	51·7	36	96·8
35/64	0·546875	13·8906	0·8	20·32	8	0·31496	130	54·4	38	100·4
9/16	0·5625	14·2875	0·9	22·86	9	0·35433	135	57·2	40	104
37/64	0·578125	14·6844	1	25·4	10	0·39370	140	60·0	42	107·6
19/32	0·59375	15·0812	2	50·8	11	0·43307	145	62·8	44	112·2
39/64	0·609375	15·4781	3	76·2	12	0·47244	150	65·6	46	114·8
5/8	0·625	15·8750	4	101·6	13	0·51181	155	68·3	48	113·4
41/64	0·640625	16·2719	5	127·0	14	0·55118	160	71·1	50	122
21/32	0·65625	16·6687	6	152·4	15	0·59055	165	73·9	52	125·6
43/64	0·67185	17·0656	7	177·8	16	0·62992	170	76·7	54	129·2
11/16	0·6875	17·4625	8	203·2	17	0·66929	175	79·4	56	132·8
45/64	0·703125	17·8594	9	228·6	18	0·70866	180	82·2	58	136·4
23/32	0·71875	18·2562	10	254·0	19	0·74803	185	85·0	60	140
47/64	0·734375	18·6531	11	279·4	20	0·78740	190	87·8	62	143·6
3/4	0·75	19·0500	12	304·8	21	0·82677	195	90·6	64	147·2
49/64	0·765625	19·4469	13	330·2	22	0·86614	200	93·3	66	150·8
25/32	0·78125	19·8437	14	355·6	23	0·90551	205	96·1	68	154·4
51/64	0·796875	20·2406	15	381·0	24	0·94488	210	98·9	70	158
13/16	0·8125	20·6375	16	406·4	25	0·98425	212	100·0	75	167
53/64	0·828125	21·0344	17	431·8	26	1·02362	215	101·7	80	176
27/32	0·84375	21·4312	18	457·2	27	1·06299	220	104·4	85	185
55/64	0·859375	21·8281	19	482·6	28	1·10236	225	107·2	90	194
7/8	0·875	22·2250	20	508·0	29	1·14173	230	110·0	95	203
57/64	0·890625	22·6219	21	533·4	30	1·18110	235	112·8	100	212
29/32	0·90625	23·0187	22	558·8	31	1·22047	240	115·6	105	221
59/64	0·921875	23·4156	23	584·2	32	1·25984	245	118·3	110	230
15/16	0·9375	23·8125	24	609·6	33	1·29921	250	121·1	115	239
61/64	0·953125	24·2094	25	635·0	34	1·33858	255	123·9	120	248
31/32	0·96875	24·6062	26	660·4	35	1·37795	260	126·6	125	257
63/64	0·984375	25·0031	27	690·6	36	1·41732	265	129·4	130	266

How to read the remaining tables in this section

Read the 'tens' in the first or last column and the units along the top. Eg, to convert 25 feet to metres read down to 20 and across to 5 = 7·62 m.

Feet to Metres

(ft)	(m) 0	1	2	3	4	5	6	7	8	9	
—		0·305	0·610	0·914	1·219	1·524	1·829	2·134	2·438	2·743	—
10	3·048	3·353	3·658	3·962	4·267	4·572	4·877	5·182	5·486	5·791	10
20	6·096	6·401	6·706	7·010	7·315	7·620	7·925	8·230	8·534	8·839	20
30	9·144	9·449	9·754	10·058	10·363	10·668	10·973	11·278	11·582	11·887	30
40	12·192	12·497	12·802	13·106	13·411	13·716	14·021	14·326	14·630	14·935	40
50	15·240	15·545	15·850	16·154	16·459	16·764	17·069	17·374	17·678	17·983	50
60	18·288	18·593	18·898	19·202	19·507	19·812	20·117	20·422	20·726	21·031	60
70	21·336	21·641	21·946	22·250	22·555	22·860	23·165	23·470	23·774	24·079	70
80	24·384	24·689	24·994	25·298	25·603	25·908	26·213	26·518	26·822	27·127	80
90	27·432	27·737	28·042	28·346	28·651	28·956	29·261	29·566	29·870	30·175	90

Square Inches to Square Centimetres

(sq. in. or in.²)	(cm²) 0	1	2	3	4	5	6	7	8	9	
—		6·452	12·903	19·355	25·807	32·258	38·710	45·161	51·613	58·065	—
10	64·516	70·968	70·420	83·871	90·323	96·774	103·226	109·678	116·129	122·581	10
20	129·033	135·484	141·936	148·387	154·839	161·291	167·742	174·194	180·646	187·097	20
30	193·549	200·000	206·452	212·904	219·355	225·807	232·259	238·710	245·162	251·613	30
40	258·065	264·517	270·968	277·420	283·871	290·323	296·775	303·226	309·678	316·130	40
50	322·581	329·033	335·485	341·936	348·388	354·839	361·291	367·743	374·194	380·646	50
60	387·098	393·549	400·001	406·452	412·904	419·356	425·807	432·259	438·711	445·162	60
70	451·614	458·065	464·517	470·969	477·420	483·872	490·324	496·775	503·227	509·678	70
80	516·130	522·582	529·033	535·485	541·937	548·388	554·840	561·291	567·743	574·195	80
90	580·646	587·098	593·550	600·001	606·453	612·904	619·356	625·808	632·259	638·711	90

Cubic Inches to Cubic Centimetres

(cu in. or in³)	(cc or cm³) 0	1	2	3	4	5	6	7	8	9	
—		16·387	32·774	49·162	65·549	81·936	98·323	114·710	131·097	147·484	—
10	163·872	180·259	196·646	213·033	229·420	245·808	262·195	278·582	294·969	311·356	10
20	327·743	344·130	360·518	376·905	393·292	409·679	426·066	442·453	458·841	475·228	20
30	491·615	508·002	524·389	540·776	557·164	573·551	589·938	606·325	622·712	639·099	30
40	655·486	671·874	688·261	704·648	721·035	737·422	753·809	770·197	786·584	802·971	40
50	819·358	835·745	852·132	868·520	884·907	901·294	917·681	934·068	950·455	966·843	50
60	983·230	999·617	1016·004	1032·391	1048·778	1065·166	1081·553	1097·940	1114·327	1130·714	60
70	1147·101	1163·489	1179·876	1196·263	1212·650	1229·037	1245·424	1261·811	1278·199	1294·586	70
80	1310·973	1327·360	1343·747	1360·134	1376·522	1392·909	1409·296	1425·683	1442·070	1458·457	80
90	1474·845	1491·232	1507·619	1524·006	1540·393	1556·780	1573·168	1589·555	1605·942	1622·329	90

Pounds to Kilogrammes

(lb)	(kg) 0	1	2	3	4	5	6	7	8	9	
—		0·454	0·907	1·361	1·814	2·268	2·722	3·175	3·629	4·082	—
10	4·536	4·990	5·443	5·897	6·350	6·804	7·257	7·711	8·165	8·618	10
20	9·072	9·525	9·979	10·433	10·886	11·340	11·793	12·247	12·701	13·154	20
30	13·608	14·061	14·515	14·968	15·422	15·876	16·329	16·783	17·237	17·690	30
40	18·144	18·597	19·051	19·504	19·958	20·412	20·865	21·319	21·772	22·226	40
50	22·680	23·133	23·587	24·040	24·494	24·948	25·401	25·855	26·308	26·762	50
60	27·216	27·669	28·123	28·576	29·030	29·484	29·937	30·391	30·844	31·298	60
70	31·751	32·205	32·659	33·112	33·566	34·019	34·473	34·927	35·380	35·834	70
80	36·287	36·741	37·195	37·648	38·102	38·855	39·009	39·463	39·916	40·370	80
90	40·823	41·277	41·731	42·184	42·638	43·091	43·545	43·998	44·452	44·906	90

Index